# Heart Flip

Molly Fisk
Editor

Julie Gamberg, Robin Jacobson,
Karen Lewis & Michael McLaughlin
Field Editors

2001
California Poets in the Schools
Statewide Anthology

CALIFORNIA
POETS IN THE
SCHOOLS

Cover art by 4th & 5th grade students from the Buena Vista
Alternative Elementary School, San Francisco: Carlos, Daniel,
Elena, Ericka, Fiona, Jesse, Lauren, Leo, Montana, Oscar,
Ostmar & Zoe. Poetry/art teacher (through a grant from the
San Francisco Education Fund on the Visual Art of Literacy):
Brenda Nasio; Classroom teacher: Liliana Valle.

Cover design by Susanna Wilson & Associates, Grass Valley, CA

Book design by Wordsworth, San Geronimo Valley, CA

Printing by McNaughton & Gunn, Saline, MI

ISBN # 0-939927-18-7

*This anthology is dedicated to*
*Mary Vradelis, our Executive Director,*
*with gratitude for her vision and leadership.*

California Poets in the Schools is grateful to the hundreds of individuals, foundations, and agencies who graciously offer their support:

Brian Smith & Alison McLean
Christopher & Gail Mead
Jennifer Miller
Karin Moe
Delia Moon
Carmel S. D. Naraval
Chris Olander
Felicia Oldfather
Reathe Joy Oliver
Mary Pallares
B.A. Pasley
Allon Rafael
Laurie & Marc Recordon
Stephen Rentmeesters
Judith Ghidinelli & Sharon Page
   Ritchie
Ivy & Leigh Robinson
Lake & Carlos Rodriguez
Susan Roegiers
Elizabeth Rosenberg
Faye Rosenzweig
Leo & Deborah Ruth
Craig & Cheryl Sattervall
Pamela & Harold Schneider
Don Shanley
Beth Thomasy & Dan Shvodian
Peter & Mardine Sibley
Kathleen Soto
David Spina
Lani Steele
Sol Stern
Susan Stern
Gretchen Stone
James Strait, M.D.
Roselyn Swig
Edith & Robert Tannenbaum
David & Susan Terris
Celeste Teters
Jean-Louise Thacher
Quincy Troupe
Greg & Kathy Moe & Jon Watson
Karen Wendel
Eva & Mike West
Jonathan Halperin & Felicia Wong
Janet Young

**AND**
100's of California schools, teachers,
   and administrators
100's of CPITS members
10's of 1000's of K-12 students
   throughout California and their
   families

**We wish to acknowledge the support of the following Government, Corporate and Foundation supporters who have made our poetry residencies, anthologies, and conferences possible.**
California Arts Council
California Casualty Group
Chase Manhattan Foundation
Community Foundation of Santa
   Barbara
Fair Isaac Fund
Frank Foundation
Good Works Foundation
Grove Consultants International
Walter and Elise Haas Fund
Judith Stronach Fund of the
   Vanguard Foundation
Marin Community Foundation
Men's Wearhouse
The Minneapolis Foundation
Miranda Lux Foundation
National Endowment for the Arts
Orrick, Herrington and Sutcliffe LLP
The David & Lucille Packard
   Foundation
Potrero Nuevo Fund
San Francisco Arts Commission
San Francisco Department of
   Children, Youth and their Families
Silver Giving Foundation
Starbucks Foundation
Stern Foundation
St. Paul Companies and the
   Insurance Industry Charitable
   Fund
The ArtCouncil, Inc.
Valley Foundation
Dean Witter Foundation
Zellerbach Family Fund
Charlotte & Arthur Zitrin Foundation

California

Arts Council

NATIONAL
ENDOWMENT
FOR THE ARTS

# TABLE OF CONTENTS

# Introduction
## At Home in the World

When I returned to poetry, I knew I had come home. I had always enjoyed hearing and reading poems; I had even written some poems when I was in elementary and high school. I doubted if my poems were any good, though, and I went on to become preoccupied with many other things in my life. I sensed something was missing, but it was some time before I realized that I missed a sense of being at home in the world—feeling I was a unique and necessary part of the world, feeling I was connected to everyone in it and every thing.

But when I began writing and reading poems again, I realized not only something about my place in the world, but about how the world is at home in me—how nothing that is outside of me doesn't also exist inside me, how the world becomes meaningful through my efforts to make sense of it. What does poetry have to do with this? As fifth-grader Davis Finch suggests in "Poetry Is" (see page 33), poetry moves us from the initial observation of experiences to the imaginative making sense of them, and then on to the use of our imaginations to transform events and experiences. It reminds us that we have the capacity to use words, sound, and rhythm to create the world in ways that let us appreciate being alive more intensely. By doing this, we connect ourselves to everything else that lives, and we come to feel a sense of being at home.

How fortunate we all are that we have poetry in our lives! And how fortunate we are to have the following poems to read, keep, and return to later. These poems come out of some very vital experiences of children and their teachers across this state. The poems range from animated descriptions of the California landscape to some thoughtful reflections on the natures of poetry, from considerations of social relations and politics to the equally complex worlds of the self and the family, and from the celebratory to the frightening to the painful. They point out how rich and various human experiences are, and how nothing of those experiences is finally alien and unspeakable.

There are all kinds of paths that lead us away from being most alive. And, being most alive doesn't look the same for everybody. But finding our ways home seems to take most people all of their lives, for there are always new homes to find; and when we find them, we have to arrive over and over again. The poetry in this anthology helps remind us that every poem is a journey—some poet's returning to the blank page to discover where it is we are supposed to go.

*Forrest Hamer*
*Oakland, June, 2001*

## Editor's Note
## Flipping Out

I hope your hearts flip over this book of poems, as moving and diverse a selection from students throughout California as I've seen. I hope the writing of these children opens some of the locked doors in the hearts of readers and gets the ink flowing in the pens of poet-teachers, too. I know there are great lines here that have inspired me.

We had some adventures in the making of this book, including finding a title after the word "graffiti," which some of us liked, was ruled out because it didn't seem to be an appropriate artform for our organization to promote. We — the Four Fearless Field Editors: Karen Lewis, Robin Jacobson, Julie Gamberg, Michael McLaughlin, and me — read through hundreds of submissions to pick these 78 student poems, a job which is not a day at the beach, let me tell you! I always want to make the book twice as long.

I asked my nephew Nico, aged 19 and *very* cool, whether the phrase "heart flip" — from Freddie Shield's poem about skateboarding — was a common term that I, being decrepit and out-of touch, might not have heard before. But he'd never heard it either. We decided it must just be one of those magical phrases that sticks in your mind and makes a home there, so it was chosen to be this year's title.

And then came my favorite part: balancing umpteen plates in the air to get the graphics done and approved by the board; the printing scheduled; the copy put on disk and desk-topped (which is *not* a verb but never mind); the corrected spelling of last names and teachers' names entered; figuring out which towns are in which counties; checking and rechecking so we don't leave anyone out; copy-editing bluelines at the final hour and then, deep breath, getting those lovely cardboard boxes with real books in them back from the printer. And this year, in time for the conference in September. To my knowledge, no one had to take any tranquilizers in the process.

But last year I forgot some very important people, and so my apologies and many thanks 365 days later to the excellent Field Editors from 2000: Fernando C. Castro, Christine Irving, Perie Longo and Mitsuye Yamada.

None of this can be accomplished by me just sitting here on my living room floor surrounded by piles of poems. It takes Karl Frauhammer sending pricing quotes from McNaughton & Gunn in Michigan; and Susanna Wilson figuring out which font to use on the title; and Larry and Barbara Brauer asking if I really want to spell *heartt* with two "t"s. It takes Mary Vradelis okaying my haphazard budget and checking to see how many books were printed last year; and Greg McComb e-mailing me the list of donors in alphabetical order; and Helen Vradelis sending out more permission forms to all the poet-teachers who lost them (including me). It takes a dedicated volunteer board of directors agreeing that yellow is good for the cover (although I thought it was pale pea green and they'd hate it). It takes every one of our generous donors whose tens or thousands of dollars paid for the whole shebang. And it takes every poet-teacher we have, going into classrooms and giving their hearts, and all those students writing wonderful poems.

I'd say it takes a village, but Hilary Clinton already said that, and besides, we're talking about the whole state of California. It takes a bunch of people who love kids and words and who are willing to work hard so this can happen.

I am grateful to be among them.

*Molly Fisk*
*Nevada City, June, 2001*

# STUDENT POEMS

## AFTER THE RAIN

There was a
fish cloud
in the sky
and it was
swimming
towards us.

It had a
curved tail.
Its mouth
was open
and
it was eating
the sky.

**Zoe Lemieux, First Grade**
*Weathersfield Elementary, Thousand Oaks*
*Jeneen Vetrovec, Classroom teacher*
*Lucia Lemieux, Poet-Teacher*

## THE SOFTEST THING

The softest thing in the world
is a ghost. A ghost looks like
a hole in the air and sounds
like snow falling.

**Amanda Parra, First Grade**
*Central School, San Diego County*
*Elaine Porter, Classroom teacher*
*Johnnierenee Nelson, Poet-Teacher*

## INTERESTING

Are books
And the smiling moon
    green crickets
    seeds that grow
    the waves at the beach
And the clouds in the sky
    a map
And a big yak

The tip of a pencil,
A heart-shaped rock.

**Annie-Kate Wagner, Second Grade**
*Loma Vista Elementary, Ventura*
*Gloria Moore, Classroom teacher*
*Joyce Lombard, Poet-Teacher*

## MY DAD

My dad is like a secret
that I never could keep.
He's like a wolf howling at night.
His love is like an army
fighting for their country.
His happiness is a cheetah
running with his cubs into the horizon.
His trust like a hawk swooping for its prey.

Now when I go to Yosemite
the world stops turning
the man on the moon stops fishing
the sun stops shining
the moon stops coming up

the crickets stop chirping
and God stops making it rain.
The horses stop galloping
and the fish stop swimming
and the moon stops talking to the sun.

But I am thankful that I got to spend
all those wonderful seven years
bike riding across the Valley with my dad
and going to the beach when it was foggy
and going to the pool in the middle of
a hot, muggy day when we went on a hike
that led up to a man-made pond
that seemed as big as a creek
and we saw lots of fish, our favorite:
the rainbow one with gold on its tips.

I wish that my dad could be here.
But for all I know he's hiking
Mt. Everest right now with a friend.
His hands are like vines or like a black river
rushing through the heather lands,
his eyes like a crow squawking at sunrise
his feet like tanks carrying missiles toward their bases
his hair like a dark, dark basement in the September rain.
His heart, a tropical ocean with a storm of fish
just waiting to be caught.

Rachael Masoud, Second Grade
*Wade Thomas School, San Anselmo*
*Monica Dewey, Classroom teacher*
*Karen Benke, Poet-Teacher*

## My Family in Winters, CA

My father is a California poppy
  climbing up blue and purple walls,
  invading Putah Creek.

My mother is a palm tree with lots of branches
  outside the Buckhorn,
  with a dragonfly flying around her.

My sister is Cody's Market
  with a lot of honey pots on the roof,
  with ice also on the roof.

I am a salmon in a purple cherry tree
  with poison oak and honey
  on the bottoms of the cherries.

**Jessica Cortez, Third Grade**
*Waggoner Elementary, Yolo County*
*Vicky Catalan, Classroom teacher*
*Maria Melendez, Poet-Teacher*

# THE RIVERS

The rivers are ice.
Crystals of gold.
My life to the animals.
The dancing tornadoes in a tree.
Sky of dreams. The winter
rivers rose in the night sky.
The pearls in the oceans.
The stories of an ocean.
The sound of the
        rushing river in the stars.
The life
        of the animals
                falls down to you.

**Stephanie Marie Ong, Third Grade**
*West Portal School, San Francisco*
*Gwen McRoberts, Classroom teacher*
*Susan Terence, Poet-Teacher*

# THE ANIMALS OF MY FEELINGS

There is a horse in me
It is a beautiful butterscotch
Yellow palomino
With hair flapping
In the wind
This beautiful horse
Is my strength.

There is an owl in me
A feathery silver-black-gold owl
While its calls of wisdom
Go forth to the moon
This theatrical bird is
My powerful wisdom.

There is a red bull in me
An angry raging mad bull
Who only gives out the
Greatest anger
This is my strong anger.

There is a butterfly in me
A wonderful yellow-blue butterfly
While its wings flap
Through the spring forest
This lets out my happiness.

There is a unicorn in me
A silver-blue unicorn
It sends out happiness
Through valleys
This is the ride to my heart.

There is a person in me
A person who has
Lots of feelings
Inside her
This is the path
To my feelings.

Olivia Notter, Third Grade
*Ocean View School, Albany*
*Tracy Lohman, Classroom teacher*
*Judith Tannenbaum, Poet-Teacher*

## SCENE

Sky
with black everywhere
The sky
sprinkling snow
Everywhere
filled with the color of swans
swans flying
in the sky of cold snow
souls of plants rising.

Peter Yu, Third Grade
*Lakeshore School, San Francisco*
*Jacklyn Gorman, Classroom teacher*
*Grace Grafton, Poet-Teacher*


## WHITE MAKES ME THINK

White makes me wonder
should I color blue
and taste a salty ocean?
Should I color purple
and see a sea urchin?
Should I color green
and hear a soccer game in the park?
White makes me think.

Carl Read, Third Grade
*Hearst Elementary School, San Diego County*
*Jean Feinstein, Classroom teacher*
*Celia Sigmon, Poet-Teacher*

# I Change

My eyes change whistle blue like the
moon. My teeth change shiny white like
a shooting star. My eyebrows change
lucky brown.

Rebecca Caauso, Third Grade
*Dana Grey Elementary, Fort Bragg*
*Josyln Bartlett, Classroom teacher*
*Hannah Clapsadle, Poet-Teacher*


# The Magic Fish

It makes me think of the queer
noise on the ocean floor and the
quiet sea hitting the ocean floor
and the fish floating in water and
the magic fish turning the
ocean gold every time the
sun goes down and the people
are in their beds
sleeping. The sea is gold
and all fish are gold
and once again the people
are awake and the
sea is the way it was.

Jake Presler, Third Grade
*Dana Grey Elementary, Fort Bragg*
*Dale Perkins, Classroom teacher*
*Hannah Clapsadle, Poet-Teacher*

## SECRET LAKE

The lake from shoes.
The lake from dreams.
My lake hidden in the hills.
Always full moons
always clear sky.
Sun rising orange,
sun setting pink
drifting away to the night.
The current so calm
the water so warm
and the birds always singing.
No one knows about the lake
except for me and the fish.

**Michael Curatalo, Fourth Grade**
*Mt. View School, Santa Barbara*
*Beth Wagner, Classroom teacher*
*Lois Klein, Poet-Teacher*

## What's Inside a Star?

Happy streams of light running freely
over the cool depths of outer space.
A cat's eyes,
an eagle's beak,
half of the pizza I ate last September.
A mind that covers the universe,
an imagination that takes all.
Time that keeps on rolling,
a life that needs to be shared.
A spell that hasn't been broken for 30 years,
my name spelled in every way.

Asher King Abramson, Fourth Grade
*Marin Horizons Elementary School, Marin County*
*Annie Gordon, Classroom teacher*
*Prartho Sereno, Poet-Teacher*

# THE BOOK

*(a dream, after Magritte)*

Where am I?
I question myself.
All I did was open a book,
but now I am wading
in a waist-high field
of grass with a yellow flower
gleaming like the sun
with a golden peach in the center.
I run to it but get nowhere
hearing it tease me with
its whisper of rain, hail, fog
and suddenly I'm hanging
in the sky with all the letters
of the alphabet. I grab onto
an "r" and realize we are
falling like rain. I hear it
chanting its charm of soup.
As I'm pulled into the next page
I hear a tinkling bell of a shop.
I am sitting on a red cushion
next to glasses with red button
eyes. I see my mom come in
and realize *I'm tiny.* I call
for her but all that comes
out of my mouth is a squeak
of snail shells. I had many
other adventures and heard
other charms, but these
were my favorites.

Roxanne McKee, Fourth Grade
*Buena Vista Alternative Elementary School, San Francisco*
*Courtney Cook, Classroom teacher*
*Brenda Nasio, Poet-Teacher*

# THE RAT

One small
but strong.
One fast
and smooth.
Swift creature
the rat.
Step by step
running across the kitchen floor.
Jet black eyes
shining in the moonlight
like crystals.
Going through tunnels
beside the wall.
Thick rough tail
bumping against cabinet doors.
Fur smooth as pearls
Small and fierce
Who rides the floor
as smooth as the wind?

Julia Plotts, Fourth Grade
*Ocean View School, Albany*
*Bridget Priest, Classroom teacher*
*Judith Tannenbaum, Poet-Teacher*

## JEALOUSY

Jealousy—an
earthquake of hatred
a stampede of madness
big wanting huge, huge wanting
large, large wanting enormous
    and so it goes on
Jealousy is high yet low
    yet middle class
I can't make out the color
that's flowing through my
head. I'd say a blue yellow
green and red purple pink
a leopard wanting jaguar
jaguar wanting tiger and it
goes on and on
like wind fighting the
clouds.

**Annie Yoss, Fourth Grade**
*Manor School, Fairfax*
*Mary Acord, Classroom teacher*
*Albert DeSilver, Poet-Teacher*

# THE TONGUE OF SPIKES

The names never hurt me.
It's the sharpness of the tongue,
the sound of nails scratching a chalkboard,
the journey to the golden rays
of sunlight and warmth
shadows shouting a nightmare scream.
Fifteen wild Decembers chill
my bones and shrink my skin.
The flame runs under my skin
to fight back the ignorant
armies clashing in the dead of
night.

Leo Clare do Ceu, Fourth Grade
*McNear Elementary, Petaluma*
*Kathie Rose, Classroom teacher*
*Terry Ehret, Poet-Teacher*

# How to Be a Rock

You gotta be hard
even if you don't want to.
You gotta eat minerals.
You gotta be used to
being bored.
You gotta get used to
being on the run
from the quarry.
You gotta learn to
hold your breath when
a child throws you
into a stream.

James Voss, Fourth Grade
*Mt. View School, Santa Barbara*
*Ms. Robinson, Classroom teacher*
*Lois Klein, Poet-Teacher*

## THE LOCKED DOORS TO FREEDOM

*(dedicated to Chinese immigrants detained at Angel Island)*

I am a 9-year-old girl.
My heavenly dreams were crushed by stone.
My future had been blown back to China by the blue winds of
wails.
I am not hurt outside, but deep inside.
I am destroyed by broken crystals and diamonds.
I came here to the land of freedom,
but what I found were cloudy skies and no way out
of the dull gloom and prison bars. At night, my blankets
are stone cold—no matter how hot it is.
My heart is struck with screams and terror.
It can never be brightened with sunlight.
I wish I were back in China
where life was hard
but better than this nightmare.

**Delia Sie, Fourth Grade**
*Ulloa Elementary, San Francisco*
*Edna Kwan, Classroom teacher*
*Susan Terence, Poet-Teacher*

## SHADOW SPIRITS

A life is not only single but
it's double just like the wind flowing through
your mind like a snake in the dark
shadows of the trees that grow like buildings
in the sun. The workers lie down for a rest
but as they do the spirits arise and fly.

Chris Kensinger, Fifth Grade
*Claire Lilienthal School, San Francisco*
*Ms. Gustufson, Classroom teacher*
*Gail Newman, Poet-Teacher*


## UNTITLED

Why a person in the center of others feels like
an outsider along with the followers.

Why she feels devoted to others but they take her for
granted.

Why when she states the truth others brush it away like
unwanted dust.

Why are looks and boys so important, but friendships are like
side orders in a large meal.

Why does one person have power over all the rest,
and others are brave enough to not follow a soul.

Annie McGee, Fifth Grade
*Claire Lilienthal School, San Francisco*
*Mr. Drayne, Classroom teacher*
*Gail Newman, Poet-Teacher*

## GRANDMA'S PB COOKIES

My
grandma
always
lights
my
dark
hallways
and even
leads me
to the
other
side.
She
is the
water
of my
ocean,
the music
of my
radio
and I'm
the
peanut butter
of her
peanut butter cookies.

Jonathon Coney, Fifth Grade
*Lincoln Acres Elementary, San Diego*
*Susan Braden, Classroom teacher*
*Celia Sigmon, Poet-Teacher*

# FAMILY REUNIONS AT MY ABUELA'S HOUSE

Family reunions
at my abuela's house
with all 10 cousins
from Cuba
where people are
dancing
in the night
in the streets

We eat hot fluffy steamed
white rice
with juicy chicken

We play hide and seek
in the hot garage
for 3 hours . . .
My cousin, Dustin,
always last to be found.
He hides in the
smallest places.

We tell jokes,
jump on the bed,
run in the backyard
like crazy jumping monkeys
with no socks or shoes

running into space
over the stars and moon.

Chris Colbert, Fifth grade
*West Portal School, San Francisco*
*Ken Krause, Classroom teacher*
*Susan Terence, Poet-Teacher*

## My Non-Blood Brother

My brother is superman on a skateboard.
He is taller than me,
so he can land
the harder tricks.

I can't wait until he
lands a heart flip
because I know it will come
from his heart.

When he lands a smooth kick flip
And an easy 50/50 grind,
I am proud.
He is, he is, he is not
my blood brother,

But he is my best friend
and I love him
for it.

**Freddie Shields, Fifth Grade**
*Richard Bard Elementary School, Port Hueneme*
*Mrs. Sides, Classroom teacher*
*Lucia Lemieux, Poet-Teacher*

## WHEN I LAUGH

When I laugh,
ten blue monkeys
play trumpets in the garbage can.

**Carlos Ibarra, Fifth Grade**
*Ramon Tafoya Elementary, Woodland*
*Mrs. Townsend, Classroom teacher*
*Eve West Bessier, Poet-Teacher*


## WHEN I AM MAD

When I am mad,
Nine-million red sharks
swim in the junk yard.

**Bryan Gonzalez, Fifth Grade**
*Ramon Tafoya Elementary, Woodland*
*Mrs. Townsend, Classroom teacher*
*Eve West Bessier, Poet-Teacher*


## WHEN I WRITE POEMS

When I write poems,
41 red horses
eat ice cream under the bed.

**Ariel Stephens, Fifth Grade**
*Ramon Tafoya Elementary, Woodland*
*Mrs. Townsend, Classroom teacher*
*Eve West Bessier, Poet-Teacher*

## POETRY IS

Poetry is the way rain falls on the
street, Poetry is the way clouds
float, Poetry is the way mothers
peek on their darkest children,
Poetry is the way trees whistle
in the breeze, Poetry is the
way songs move through
your head, Poetry is the way
good dreams conquer your
nightmares.

**Davis Finch, Fifth Grade**
*Claire Lilienthal School, San Francisco*
*Mr. Drayne, Classroom teacher*
*Gail Newman, Poet-Teacher*

## IN THE COUNTRY

I see an old bridge of yellow and red.
I see a track made by wheels.
I see the sun rise over snow-coated hills.
I see a community of green pine trees.

I hear the peaceful chirps of bluebirds
in leafless trees.
I hear horses prance through paths of soil.
I hear the rooster cluck
In the Southeast Valley's yellow corn.

Green grass is a distant wish.

**Stefanie Concepcion, Fifth Grade**
*Richard Bard Elementary, Port Hueneme*
*Mrs. McLaughlin, Classroom teacher*
*Lucia Lemieux, Poet-Teacher*

## WHAT I FEEL ABOUT WAR

I hear the young boys screaming in a war,
their red blood everywhere.
I smell the flowers on their graves.
I touch their tombstones.
I see a giant field of tombstones.
I feel mornings of winter.

Mazi Tran, Fifth Grade
*McNear Elementary, Petaluma*
*Kim Ryder, Classroom teacher*
*Terry Ehret, Poet-Teacher*

## "ALMOND BLOSSOMS IN SPRINGTIME"

*(painting by Vincent Van Gogh)*

I want to tell you
about the white blossoms
that smell like springtime.

I won't forget the branches
like millions
of tiny fingers
holding each other
together.

I want to show you
how the branches
fit into the sky
like pieces of a puzzle. . . .

Sean Rogers, Fifth Grade
*West Portal School, San Francisco*
*Marina Chiappellone, Classroom teacher*
*Susan Terence, Poet-Teacher*

## DAYLIGHT SHINES

Daylight is shining in
A glass jar with
Old brown leaves.

**Dao Xiong, Fifth Grade**
*Lincoln Elementary School, Humboldt*
*Arthur Hand, Classroom teacher*
*Daniel Zev Levinson, Poet-Teacher*


## REMEMBERING

A feather white as bones
lying on the black and white gravel
beside a heart-shaped rock
next to a branch.

The ground makes me think
I'm in the mountains hunting
through the woods and the feather
makes me remember my old bird Tweety.

The picture reminds me of what
I did in the past. In ancient days
Native Americans worshipped
the heart shape that stands for love
and feathers that stand for courage
but most of all the sticks
that mean strength and power.

**Edgardo Nave, Fifth Grade**
*Lincoln Acres Elementary, San Diego*
*Sue Braden, Classroom teacher*
*Celia Sigmon, Poet-Teacher*

## ODE TO THE PEPPERS

The pepper
red like a dark lipstick
hot like the sun
burns you
but still
so innocent
the skin like an old hand
innocent
so skinny
has a sense of humor
hot hot hot
I dare you, take a bite
a little bit
innocence
*abuela tu mano es*
*como un chile*
*caliente caliente caliente*

**Taty Gutierrez, Fifth Grade**
*Jefferson School, San Francisco*
*Kim Probst, Classroom teacher*
*Susan Sibbet, Poet-Teacher*

## Soft Love

how the wind blows
in my body in this wonderful place
of land

blowing through my face
smelling hot red roses

touching and playing in
the cold wind of love

hearing the wind
sounding like a bird singing

looks like a drop
of water in my cup

**Paul Padaoan, Fifth Grade**
*Bessie Carmichael Elementary School, San Francisco*
*Elzaida Alcaide, Classroom Teacher*
*Julie Gamberg, Poet-Teacher*

# MISTY NIGHT

*(poem in two voices)*

*(Contralto or alto tenor voice)*           *(Soprano voice)*

*(Alone)*
Fog is rolling
Fog is drifting
Fog that shrouds
the city view, oh

*(With soprano)*
Fog is floating
Through the raindrops              *(Soprano start)*
Blown by wind and                 Raindrops dripping
Pierced by treetops               Through the night time
                                  Lightning strike,
Swish! The trees sway             and thunder rolls
Drip! The rain falls
Donk! The rain flows              On the drainpipe
Through the drainpipe             wind plays drums, oh
                                  Misty night, I lie awake
Swish! Drip! Donk! Tonk!
Birds fluffed up for warmth       Crash! Thonk! Weather
Caw! Caw! Angry raven             Swish, blow, windy
Swish, Drip, Swish, Drip          Wet outside, cozy within, oh

          Fog
                                  Misty night, I lie awake

                                  Rain
                                        Rain
                                             Rain
                                                  Rain

Susan Kane, Fifth Grade
*Jefferson School, San Francisco*
*Kathleen Loughlin, Classroom teacher*
*Susan Sibbet, Poet-Teacher*

## ACTION HAIKU

Flying through the air
Hot pavement at the skatepark
Hitting the ground, hard

**Matt Bair, Sixth Grade**
*Piner Elementary, Sonoma*
*Mr. Jordan, Classroom teacher*
*Penelope La Montagne, Poet-Teacher*


## POETRY

Crashing, rumbling, roaring
Over the cliffs to break against the rocks,
The muddy gray water slowing down,
To the deep bluegreen pool where fat
trout play and dragonflies hover.
The trickling becomes the river when you
        can't jump over it,
Racing down to the lake faster than sound.
The stone-faced sturgeon slithers in the dark,
And the quick-witted heron stares,
The dead fish lie rotting on the sand,
Their stench attracting mayflies,
The osprey dives, talons like daggers,
The rattlesnake seems to walk on water
        as it pursues the gopher on the opposite bank.
Cat eyes blink while sipping the water,
Telltale footprints in the mud,
The river still flows downstream,
Hearing all, feeling nothing.

**Liberty Herring, Sixth Grade**
*Seven Hills School, Nevada City*
*Jim McQuiston, Classroom teacher*
*Molly Fisk, Poet-Teacher*

## TUXEDO

Just a whisper of a sound, the soft
pad of a paw, stepping on the hard
wood floor. Just the ghost of a form
sliding through the moonlight. The
light touch of fur, like a cold soft
cloth, then away to the floor. The
dark form sitting in the moonlight,
sitting in the darkness, fading away,
drifting away, like the ghost of a
ship, not to return.

**Rein Aaron, Sixth Grade**
*Mendocino Middle School, Mendocino*
*Ann Jenks, Classroom Teacher*
*Scott Meltsner, Poet-Teacher*

## UNTITLED

My father left a map
that I can't understand.
He left a path that I can't see.
He is very different than me.
My brother follows his footsteps.
My father left stairs
that are too steep. He lives
on a leaf that I can't climb.
I have to battle to know
my father. He has not left
a rhythm for me to listen.
His bones are strong as gold.

**Sean Madison, Sixth Grade**
*San Miguel Elementary School, Santa Rosa*
*Margery Egge, Classroom teacher*
*Arthur Dawson, Poet-Teacher*

## CURFEW IN SRI LANKA

I'm in a small island in the east side.
I'm on a road where I'm not supposed to be.
I hear machine guns firing off.
I see people die and fall onto
the ground.
I hear time bombs and all sorts
of bombs being fired off.
I hear babies cry I hear mothers cry
and fathers cry.
I see people run.
I see army soldiers jump off their trucks
and run with their weapons.
I see tanks all around us.
I hear metal slugs being fired off.
I see a little kid who doesn't have a family
and lights a firework
and gets hurt.
This is a place where I'm not supposed
to be.

Nivan Jayawardene, Sixth Grade
*Cold Spring School, Santa Barbara*
*Tami Hall, Classroom teacher*
*Perie Longo, Poet-Teacher*

## INNER STRENGTH

Gone
Like the sun disappearing into the icy cold and distant
mountains
Canada geese leaving their homes and flying west
Mother coyotes abandoning their dens
Hunting for food for their young

Gone
Like aqua blue caterpillars emerging from their cocoons
becoming extraordinary butterflies
Flying away
Fish swimming away from their families
Puppies separated from loved ones at birth

Gone
Like lavender tulips being picked and taken away from a
mystical garden
Autumn leaves, bright red, shimmering orange, and soft
yellow
Blowing in the wind far away from its original tree home

She is gone
The inspiration of my life
The one who laughed with me
Cried with me
Lighting up the room
Bright green hazel eyes
Radiant as a crackling fire
Expressing my deepest secrets

She is gone
Yet, I don't choke with pain
Nor sob
I don't weep with anguish
or cry myself to sleep

She is gone
Soups are tasteless
Shrieks of laughter are painful to my ears
Love is unheard of
I am numb
Knives can pierce my bare flesh
I would feel nothing

Gone
Hazel eyes no more
Consumed by the treacherous disease of Cancer
Spirit lifting from the earth
Drifting into other worlds
Yet remaining my inner strength
Guiding me through life forever

**Michele Golabek-Goldman, Eighth Grade**
*Temple Emanuel Community Day School, Los Angeles*
*Sita Stulberg, Poet-Teacher*

## MY FAMILY

My father is a man-eating poison oak,
he is a cloud of bees covering my face.
He is a ferocious dog
standing helplessly in an empty house.

My mother is a butterfly
that flutters like a cloud.
She is scared, blending into
a lisp of grass. She has
barely healed dreams
in her full-minded head.

I am gunpowder you can hear
miles away from life,
so loud the world shatters in fear.

Love in my family hides behind a tree,
we can never see it.
It is like a squirrel in the sky.
It is a leaf fallen from the sky like a gift.

Sara Kronenberg, Sixth Grade
*Ramon S. Tafoya Elementary, Yolo County*
*Karen Dumars, Classroom teacher*
*Maria Melendez, Poet-Teacher*

# LOVE

Love is like the black of a raven's wing
As it flies into the world of love.
You can never go and find love
Love just comes and finds you.
Love is a special feeling
That you only feel if you are
In a certain kind of love
Love is the feeling you feel
As you are reading a book
And you feel like you are there
Hearing, seeing, tasting
Everything that is going on
As you read on.
Love is the boat
That lets you pass over
The sea of sadness
Without suffering.

Austin Dworaczyk, Sixth Grade
*Grizzly Hill School, Nevada County*
*Ralph Henson, Classroom teacher*
*Will Staple, Poet-Teacher*

## Untitled

The star flickers
it spins
        and collapses slowly
     through Time
it spins
        faster
faster
     Time slows as the star explodes
        in a cloud of flames,
as its surface warps and stretches

Waves of gas and heat
     fly off and around the inferno
as the envelope of time around the star
              s l o w s
to a halt.
     the last sheets of flame blow into the night.
the white-hot sphere left behind
     slowly stops spinning.

         and the flow of Time rebegins

the glowing matter
     out in intergalactic noplace never ends

to the improbability factor of
     1 to 502,894,000 and growing.
The probability of finding why this happened is
     1 to 121,212,038,889,412 and
        falling.

Reid Chandler, Sixth Grade
*Mendocino Middle School, Mendocino*
*Anne Jenks, Classroom teacher*
*Karen Lewis, Poet-Teacher*

## HOW THINGS SHAPE UP

I came from a blob of *pintura,*
                          Jalisco.
Then I came to *el biberon*
                          California,
on an *avion humana.*
I used to live in a *rebanada de pastel*
                          apartment.
I rode on my mom's twinky
                          van
          *todos las dias.*

Now I go to lasagne-shaped Tafoya Elementary.

And today, on my way to Cache Creek, I saw human-
                          shaped birds.

Antonio Novelo, Sixth Grade
*Ramon S. Tafoya Elementary, Yolo County*
*Grace Callaway, Classroom teacher*
*Maria Melendez, Poet-Teacher*

## SOLITAIRE TOGETHER

When I play solitaire
I think of her dealing
out the
cards
her pinkies up
her long fingers carefully
placing the first seven
cards
she picks up the extra
cards
flipping over 3
what is on her mind?
the wooden table is
hard, stable
I smell the ocean
and hear the waves
crashing
the brick floor sandy
she pulls her yellow shirt
down her pinkies still up
but she is not proper just
pinkies
her shorts brush her
skin her knees are bent
her skin light
she stands up
asks if her cookie noodle
wants anything
I shake my head

her gray hair is pinned to her head
in clips
she is my gray eagle and I hope it
will never change
she is old
but she is teaching me
new

Sienne Hayes, Sixth Grade
*Sunny Brae Middle School, Humboldt County*
*Andy Slavin, Classroom teacher*
*Daniel Zev Levinson, Poet-Teacher*

## TIME IS LIKE A TRAIN

Time is like a train rushing past you.
When will your train come?
Its moaning whistle speeds toward you.
It's your time to board,
and you haven't lived
a day in your life,
Waiting for the train.

Ryan Reaves, Seventh Grade
*Chico Junior High School, Butte County*
*Rachel LeDuc, Classroom teacher*
*Danielle Alexich, Poet-Teacher*

# UNTITLED

My name
started as a cow.
Grazing on the moon.
A star fell out of the sky
and killed it.
An eyeball rolled off the moon
and into the ocean on earth.
A fish ate it, and was caught
on the Isle of Labor.
A goat cut open its stomach, and
found an eyeball made of hummingbird feathers.
He took it to a sweatshop
and made a child squish it into a pancake,
and then put it in a crate
with other pieces of names,
VCRs, video cameras, party favors, high-heeled shoes.
A ship took it to Taiwan
where it turned into a sound in a bottle.
It was packed into a huge box
and shipped to South America.
A breeze opened the unlocked box,
and my name fell into a truck.
It hid in the bananas
for a long time.
The truck carried the bottle into the city to the hospital
where I
was being born,
and it flew out of the truck.
Just as I was born,
it hopped out of the bottle and into me.

Max Kuhn, Seventh Grade
*Martin Luther King School, Berkeley*
*Judith Stronach, Poet-Teacher*

## JADE NUMBERS

Fingers scuttle
up, down, up, down, the green beads.
Five, one hundred, three thousand, ten.
Eyes wander from paper to marble.
Breaths wait as the mathematician
twirls his beard.
Women's hair garnets fall
at the sight of the numbers and names.
The Emperor's son faints.
Wind waits.
Roses wither, skies fold.
Children stop running.
Wives weep at the sight.
Fans close.
Fingers continue to flip the pearly beads
sliding up and down the Jade Abacus.
"100,000 dead."
The ruckus of the leaves
dancing in the wind calms no one.

**Lea Yu, Seventh Grade**
*Mesa Verde Middle School, San Diego*
*Janet Helbock, Classroom teacher*
*Glory Foster, Poet-Teacher*

## SIC WIT IT

This poem is crazy
This poem sick in the line
Like drugs on the paper
This poem is off da hook
Like a mental patient
Without medicine
This poem is stupid
Like someone with no sense at all
Lying on the street on Monday morning
With heavy traffic coming down on him
With no mercy

In their heart wanting to kill it
With their left front tire
At a speed of
90 mph.

Jerome Martin, Seventh Grade
*Lowell Middle School, Oakland*
*Jeff Resnick, Classroom teacher*
*John Isaacson, Poet-Teacher*


## RECIPE FOR A NEW YEAR

Start
With a mossy green thought
That you can bend
And shape
Until
You have a dream.

Take that dream
and let it
F
  L
    O
    W
Between your fingers
Then wind it up
And unravel it into a bowl
Of love
With a circle of friends
Around the rim.

Then stir
And add some red, for happiness,
And stir some more, until pink, frothy bubbles
Float on the top.

Now, take the vital part of the mixture
From your soul.
Self-patience, truth, honesty, forgiveness,
Everything we love of others,
Everything we love of ourselves.
All things real,
And all things abstract, but necessary.

Last, we need hope.
And memories, happy and sad,
Serenity, calmness, trust.

Now gulp.

Don't be afraid to leave fear behind
And drink to your soul
And always be true to it.

**Danielle Spoor, Seventh Grade**
*Pacific Charter School, Mendocino County*
*David Devine, Classroom teacher*
*Blake More, Poet-Teacher*

# TO DRINK FROM AN EMPTY TEA CUP

To drink from an empty tea cup,
first you must master the self-control
to tell yourself you are drinking.
To fool your mouth into thinking the air is tea.
You must also be able to refill your cup
once you've drained it.
To pour from nothingness and yet
have your cup brimming with something
aromatic and herbal.

To lift the cup to your lips and
sip the warm, sweet, soothing nothing.
To savor the calming flavor of nothing.
To subdue your thirst with nothing.
That is to drink from an empty tea cup.

**Alex Hoyt, Eighth Grade**
*Mill Valley Middle School, Marin County*
*Gretchen Viestra, Classroom teacher*
*Prartho Sereno, Poet-Teacher*

## How to Juice Steel

Close your eyes.
Forget everything you know.
Forget about atoms and properties.
Then teach yourself about you.
Pick up the steel,
and tell yourself it's not there.
Say it over and over
until the steel cannot be felt.
Then bring the feeling of steel back
to your hand,
but don't believe it's there.
Open your eyes;
see if you can feel the thick heavy
ice cold liquid
and realize that you did not juice steel
you juiced your soul.

**Kelly Gorton, Eighth Grade**
*Davidson Middle School, Marin County*
*Justin Kielty, Classroom teacher*
*Prartho Sereno, Poet-Teacher*

## Madness

Madness sits alone in the back in his own little zone
Waiting for the person he can take off on.
He wears black jeans and a black shirt.
Doesn't like anyone he thinks is a jerk.
When you step up you're laid down.
He never flinches or frowns.
You don't matter
'Cause he don't care
You can't find love or friendship anywhere
They're stuck in a trash can down the hall
'cause madness has finally destroyed them all.

Jennifer Owens, Eighth Grade
*Lowell Middle School, Oakland*
*Catherine McFeeters, Classroom teacher*
*John Isaacson, Poet-Teacher*

## LA MASCARA DE CHISPAS

*La mascara de lumbre tiene chispas,*
*lumbre que baila y es como gotas del sol.*

*En su cara tiene gotas de lumbre,*
*rojo, anaranjado, que calienta el viento*
*que es prevenirlos.*

*Detras de la mascara hay un bosque verde*
*Con mucho oscuridad.*

*La mascara de lumbre recuerda cuando el sol sale.*

*La mascara de lumbre esconde la luz del dia.*

The mask of flame has sparks,
flames that dance and are like sundrops.

On its face it has drops of flame,
red, orange, that heat the wind
as a warning.

Behind the mask is a green forest
with deep shade.

The mask of flame remembers when the sun went away.

The mask of flame hides the light of day.

**Emilia Posada, Eighth Grade**
*Casa Familiar, San Ysidro*
*Brandon Cesmat, Poet-Teacher*

## Farmer's Market

Peach man deals in dimes
dirt seals nail to finger
thumb red as salsa.

        Cardboard case piled with
        long green beans split in corners,
        like seller's thin smile.

Seventy-one cents
clip the thorns that spiral my
newspaper-wrapped  rose.

        Bread vendor leans back
        against the wooden table
        weakens from the weight.

C a r a m e l    p o p c o r n    m a c h i n e
s t r e t c h e s    w i d e    o v e r    b o t h    r o w s
a n n i h i l a t e s    t h e    s m e l l s .

**Amelia Rosenman, Ninth Grade**
*Play on Words Program, San Francisco*
*Albert DeSilver and Dana Lomax, Poet-Teachers*

## UNTITLED

Softer than a pile of cotton t-shirts
and as burdened with color as
a new-born's mind
I would run through the aisles
with arms outstretched
to touch everything I could before
it was time to leave.
Mom would take me here
after kindergarten every now
and then when she still
made a lot of my clothes
and like the heroin-addicted
supermodels, I would touch
a wad of silk and become so
enthralled I would forget
to breathe. Mom would run
and run and call my name and I
would hide to stay with my
private gallery of colors
and textures. I have a problem,
I have a substance addiction
but what a wonderful substance it is.
It's o.k. if you give up on me.

Sara Ataiiyan, Tenth Grade
*Santa Rosa High School, Sonoma County*
*Susan Kennedy, Poet-Teacher*

## THE BRIDGE

Under the Second Street bridge is a door
that opens Pandora's Box.
Once this door opens,
the White Rabbit is on time.
Marie Antoinette gives out fish
and loaves to all who come near.
Dionysus puts the Manischevitz away
and tells the Maenads to call it a day.
The spleen-ripping, child-eating
Raiders forget the commitment to
excellence and invite the 49ers over
for incense and peppermints.
Marilyn Monroe puts on a full-length
sweatsuit while Humphrey Bogart chews
Nicoderm CQ. But when the door is closed
no change is let loose. I won't tell
if you won't. Will you?

Jeremy Moskowitz, Tenth Grade
*Santa Rosa High School, Sonoma County*
*Susan Kennedy, Poet-Teacher*

## EXTRAORDINARY SOUND

We enter the low end world.
The stage my own battlefield,
the floor my own city.
Double bass guitar
single drummer
one single snare drum.
The warmth of my fingertips
heats the ice-cold thick wound strings.
The body of my sword
enters my body as we become one.
The music flows at the beat of that snare.
POP, SNAP!!
Heads bob to each and every whack.

Nick Rappoport, Tenth Grade
*Santa Rosa High School, Sonoma County*
*Susan Kennedy, Poet-Teacher*

# Thoughts

Streaming waterfall rolling with fuchia flowers—Hawaii never
   seen
       Beads throwing glass bodies to shatter purple
Beach house adorned on cushions of sand Tide wash
Shells scattered pressed in ochre grains of warm fire
Afternoon fawn lights upon bicycle in park. Pine slits
       Crackle. A leopard makes the same sound
all over the sweet-smelling floor under trees (green tops)
with the noisy silence of silver pins falling on cotton
Let's go. Have a rose starry night opal moon
Black hair Black night Black eyes wet tears mourner
Girl. Who? Anonymous forever. Look. Graffiti—red and blue
   fuzz what a
dirty wall. What does SAC mean . . . the scrawls scream from
   the wall silhouette huddled
dejected
cold gritty sidewalk and no place to turn home
is street. CD's are like life. False. Arrest is natural.
Moonlight on the dock. Wood glazed with cream sugar pale
Reading Rainbow to you with
Mouse detectives in beige trenchcoats all pastel (oil) fish
   mystery
Whooo . . . foghorn lonely mist cross TV couch
Summer days too reruns of "Growing Pains" the eucalyptus tree
is peeking in and crack! Earthquake singing "'Tis a gift to be
   Simple" marching
together now. Smiling. Black-and-white picture. Old happy
   films. Flash.
What
Easter eggs, swimming at night, horses, sea turtles—bullet train
   of neon underground
A car parked edge of weary road jeep Bonanza-like
Zip

riding off into the sunset of the desert (Cactus!)
Smile barbecue white fences I knew it would happen
Don't forget to kiss the cook. Have more salad.
REM—the only place you can get chartreuse paper shred
  coleslaw

Nance Yuan, Tenth Grade
*Play on Words Program, San Francisco*
*Albert DeSilver and Dana Lomax, Poet-Teachers*


## VELVET BLUE

A polluted river that smells
sweeter than kiwi black sherbet
clipped the wings of a parrot
rusty metal cages detained a flowering rose
seedlings were destined and had plenty of sun
fertile soil was rarely there
train tracks donating standing ovations
warriors losing wars concealed behind a wide smile
that welcomed pain and alloyed joy
butterscotch nights could that star be her?
candle wax burns here then gone
If life's a candle where's the rain
It's drought season
suddenly disengaged from the roots
that carry water like a young girl
who retrieves velvet blue
for dinner and laundry.

Phillip De La Cruz, Eleventh Grade
*Sonoma County Juvenile Hall/Felice Unit, Sonoma County*
*Celia Lamantia, Classroom teacher*
*Penelope La Montagne, Poet-Teacher*

# GHAZAL

The green fire of the lantern hanging in the doorway
burns my eyes, my nose, my empty pages

The radio talks as if to say, "You are not alone
in your bitterness," as I lie back on the purple moon

I gesture to the geese, "Go, team, go!" but they do
not listen, only seeking the tranquility of downtown Las Vegas

Somewhere a man cuts his finger and the blue blood
that flows will feed a nation

Who cares if the "walls could talk"? They have
a never-ending conspiracy with the floors and the door
to never reveal the derivatives and integrals of life

And at 1600 Pennsylvania Avenue, the American flag
        flies proudly,
but ever so slowly dripping the blood and dreams
of a few insanely tyrannical souls

Golden $20 bills fly in the breeze, sought by all,
but only seen by "the few, the proud, the Marines"

In the distance, a tiger fights and questions its eternal destiny
of existence, and it is then that you and I
realize music is the great equalizer

A man will open his heart to a woman
and see the Garden of Eden overgrown with weeds.

Austin Moy, Eleventh Grade
*Santa Barbara Music & Arts Conservatory, Santa Barbara*
*Perie Longo, Poet-Teacher*

# NIGHTWALK

This night the fleshy elbows
and fingers of fog
ambushed their way up the valley
drowning by surprise
the hot human beacons
in milky phosphorescence.
So why not flick your thumb
down that tacky ridged plastic
and embrace the darkness?
Your vision is glass;
with time,
it ripples.The night
is a gasping hungry thing:
Feel yourself
coiled like a spring.

Jacob Clapsadle, Eleventh Grade
*Mendocino High School, Mendocino*
*Bill Lemos, Classroom teacher*
*Scott Meltsner, Poet-Teacher*

# DASH

I'm a freakin' punctuation mark
in the English language
a freakin' link between stupid words
a line, an insignificant single stroke
that is quickly done away with
fast forgotten

but at least my name isn't semicolon or comma
at least I have different meanings
to my name
turn me diagonal and poof!
I'm a back slash
put words on each side of me
and now I'm a hyphen
should I go on?

**Dash Arkenstone, Twelfth Grade**
*Aliso High School, Reseda*
*Sharon Simon, Classroom teacher*
*Fernando D. Castro, Poet-Teacher*

## My Life

My life, guns through thick and thin,
mission aborted beneath the color of my skin,
jumped into a gang since the age of twelve,
5 years later I'm by myself,
cornered in a corner but no way to get out,
fighting a struggle without a doubt,
so I surrender to my own mistakes,
facing the past is what it's gonna take,
regardless of what I've done I thank my mother
for blessing me with life same as my brother,
in and out of juvenile facilities,
compare like and as, as like is a simile.

Marvin Galvez, Twelfth Grade
*North Marin Continuation School, Marin County*
*Laura Roberts, Classroom teacher*
*Albert DeSilver, Poet-Teacher*

## Coyote in Winters

Coyote walks out in the morning and sees the sun,
                sees a big white bridge.

Coyote wishes he saw people growing from trees like oranges,
                wishes he saw a big blue ocean,
                wishes he saw some fine *niñas*.

Coyote says he is so thirsty he will drink up all of Putah Creek,
                but after five minutes his belly hurts.

Coyote plays a joke on the antique shop and stands in the
    window like he's for sale.

When Coyote is mayor of Winters, he will fill the streets with
    dancing and laughter,
                he will fill the potholes with gold.

When Coyote visits my house, he'll throw a giant block party
                and eat up all the ice cream in the freezer.
                He will be impressed by the amount of trash
                in my garbage cans.

Winters needs Coyote to remind us that towns can die,
    but nature endures.

\*\*\*

Coyote walks out in the morning and sees an orange tree,
                sees clouds smothering the hills
                as he creeps into the valley.

Coyote wishes he saw his mother yipping *bienvenidos*.

Coyote played a joke on a rabbit and pretended to be dead,
                with his legs sticking up in the air.

Coyote walked up to a crowd of people and cried wolf.

When Coyote is mayor, he'll build movie theaters
and declare every fourth day a festival of almond feasting.

When Coyote visits my house, he will clean,
                    then he will eat my cats.

Winters needs Coyote because we can get stuff done with him,
                    he makes the town brighter.

\*\*\*

Coyote walks out in the morning and sees the car wash,
                    water streaming off the shiny cars,
                        sees mosquitoes flying above the sidewalk.

Coyote wishes he saw scraps of his prey lying on the ground
                    for an easy meal.

Coyote ate insects and spit them out.

Coyote walked across the old train bridge and fell into the
    icy cold water.

Mayor Coyote howls from the overpass,
                    decides to make fences illegal.

I don't want Coyote to visit my house because I just cleaned
    and organized it.

He's dorky, but Winters needs Coyote because there are no
    other coyotes in town.

\*\*\*

Coyote walks out in the morning and sees scraps
                    of clouds hanging over walnut orchards,
                        sees his friend, the owl, sitting on an oak tree branch.

Coyote wishes he saw a field of flowers.

Coyote kicks a tree and falls to his knees,
            *El Coyote* plays a joke on his best friend.

When Coyote is mayor, he'll build a bigger high school and
    a mall;
                he'll let everyone drive a car before they turn 15.

When Coyote visits my house, we'll sit down and watch TV,
                and he will bring me a new Dodge Sport.

Winters needs Coyote because he's a survivor,
and this town has to survive a lot of different kinds of people.

**The Students of Mrs. Faye's English Class, 10th, 11th,
and 12th Grades**
*Wolfskill High School, Yolo County*
*Dorian Faye, Classroom teacher*
*Maria Melendez, Poet-Teacher*

## CALIFORNIA KANSAS

The cars pass as always in a California Kansas
the buzz of an air conditioner rattled a sleepless night
    wait until morning when it's supposed to be cool
but one day the morning came still bearing yesterday's heat
and the garbage trucks beeping the distance
and the cars pass as usual in the cracked and dusty streets of
this California Kansas.

I had a pair of ruby slippers in my bag,
left home without looking back
at my weeping mother in an airport on
a night as hot as last night

We all know how hot it gets.
We all remember last summer as
    we look for a shady place to park the car.

There wasn't any air conditioning where I went;
hot nights away from home, overcast, muggy June days

The SUVs of the USA are driving down the street as usual
I smell Degree as I lift my arms to straighten my hair
and I remember tossing, naked in an un-air-conditioned loft
bed
too hot even for sheets,
and I remember waking in the sweat I'd gone to sleep in.

But that was last year, now I have the slippers clicked
and put away, for if I ever
If I ever go looking for my heart's desire,
I won't look any further
than my own backyard,
for if it isn't there
it isn't there,
then I never really lost it to begin with.

Return to this California Kansas,
where the cornfields stretch out along
the gleaming black highway that wavers
in the heat of the distance

Now we can buy cherries again,
if we can find a shady place to park the car;
watermelons are back in season,
and the cars pass us by in the hot streets.
The steering wheel's black leather is too hot to touch
because we couldn't find a shady place to park the car

this time last year I groped for
a breeze from an Oz-bound bus window

in new heat that is so like memories
sit before the passing cars in
California Kansas.

**Hava Glick-Landes, Twelfth Grade**
*Winters High School, Yolo County*
*Elizabeth Coman, Classroom teacher*
*Maria Melendez, Poet-Teacher*

## ROASTING A NEW VISION

Before I knew of this world
Even before I was huddled within your round motel
You were there on the warm beige sand
kneeling, creating, caring, roasting fish
Out of sunset-red Tupperware, the latest craze
With its patent burp and freshness guaranteed
In a world where limited warranties outlast marriage vows
With a promise of provision, to care and love
And continually turn, not to burn one side or overcook the tail
Trying to be fair, you watched, gripped, flipped,
And let the savory, pungent, salty seaweed smoke cloud
your view
But with a clear view
One day, before I was an integer,
You would sail to a new world, scared to lose your tongue,
regardless
You stopped speaking to me in Fukyen and Tagalon
Turned the TV to Sesame Street and raised me as a hope
The steamed rice still awaits every meal
But I've learned to despise the magenta bagoong and
     mustard-orange Pinak-bet
Pass the fried chicken and zesty Hamburger Helper
Notwithstanding how I've grown with such different values
Two worlds in one abode
You forget it was your vision
On the conforming sands of the Philippine shores
Living without running water
That as you turned the tempering fish
You whispered to yourself, in a ritual of cooking and
hopeful promises

That I'd speak English and drink milk
Because before I was born
You walked the shores and dreamt of a life beyond the sunset
        In a land where I wouldn't have to work on my
            knees and fry fish

Abigail Dineros, Twelfth Grade
*Morse High School, San Diego County*
*Robert Lunsford, Classroom teacher*
*Glory Foster, Poet-Teacher*


## ODE TO BEGGARS

Inspecting from the balcony, my eyes spot a beggar.
The man is swimming through my garbage, finding treasure
        in decay.
I spin around violently and slam the sliding door.
My head shakes with irritation, wishing I had courage like
        that of the man outside.
I tear up the letter on my desk and storm away.
Rage gallops about, rejoicing over his victory in shredding
        my letter, a plea of love.

A mother gazes dreamily at her newborn, baptized in love.
I hear the baby cry desperately for nourishment, a beggar.
I sneer jealously at the bundle of blankets and turn my face
        away.
Room after room in the hospital, bodies decay,
But the baby escapes, receives a tender kiss from the sun,
        welcomed by freshness outside.
A tear of longing slithers down my cheek as I close the door.

One chance was all he needed, one open door,
One visit, if only for a moment, from love.
Fear made his body shiver as he stepped outside,

Alone, rejected, he became a beggar.
Who thought this single step outside could have saved him
    from his life's decay?
Most believed he was throwing his life away!

"Go away!"
I screeched with the piercing sound of a crow. She cowered
    as she escaped out the door,
Looking past the street's gutters, oozing with decay,
She longed for a sign of real love.
A passerby, a stranger, took pity on her, believing her to be
    a beggar.
The wind caressed her like a butterfly. She found more than
    hollow nothingness outside.

Reading the time on his golden watch, he rushed in to find
    relief from the hot sun outside.
He hoped someday to fly away
To the paradise he had cried out for like a beggar.
Closing the door,
He wondered if there was such a place of love.
He winced as he was greeted inside by the stench of the
    garbage's decay.

Searching, one lonely heart finds pearls in decay.
The sun breaks through the clouds outside.
Searching, one lonely heart finds love,
Not turned away.
Each morning a fresh chance, opening the door,
Resuming the role of a beggar.

On this planet of decay, another story a moment away.
A tale of life outside, past the death lurking behind the
    closed door,
Another story of love, another beggar.

Danielle Baratiak, Twelfth Grade
*Santa Barbara Music & Arts Conservatory, Santa Barbara*
*Perie Longo, Poet-Teacher*

# POET-TEACHER POEMS

# BLACKBOARD

I draw a poem.

A parade of candles
Sighs for a dark place.

A bellowing bass
Marks time passing.

A green tomato
Clings to ripe questions.

I draw a poem.

A raised bar chants.
Rise up and touch it.

Rain tap dances on glass.
Let it move you.

A left-handed child screams.
Accept her the way she is.

I draw a poem.

An eraser sanitizes;
Chalk-dust words kiss the wind.


Lucia Lemieux
*Ventura County*

existence feels like
a construct
of confusing complexity
where the strands of winged nature
and plastic artifice
intermingle in ways
that are not predictable
with any known formula

forget the double helix,
isosceles, trapezoid,
iambic pentameter, couplet,
equilateral, parallelogram,
mobius,

we morph
around the
ions of each other
in a universe where
children are eager
to reveal truth
where children keep their hearts
on the blood-drenched line
of civilization's battleground

a child's words create
a new language
a galactic nebula
of possibilities
where i promise you this

lost homework
shall disappear forever
from the equation
of reality
i promise you this

poetry
shall remain
an eternally true
democracy

eternally defined
eternally free

Karen Lewis
*Mendocino*

## ODE TO MY STAPLER

Little stapler how like a lion you sit
ready to chomp down on any papery prey
that falls between your jaws.
Poised for action, your metal fangs
so square and uniform, line up
one after another like good soldiers
never looking back.
I've held you in my palm
more times than I can count
gripping your rubbery underside
which seemed embarrassed to be lifted off the table,
but still, you obeyed.
Once or twice I've left you on the desk
and come down on your head
with a pounding fist, and you were good,
you joined the pages, you made them one.
But it pained me to smack so at your brow
so I will continue to lift you up
and squeeze you gently
so you can savor the penetration
through paper, and the neat folding of your staples,
the gratifying union that is your calling.

Mary Lee Gowland
*Madera*

## MY PROFESSION

It's the name that's the problem
(and of course the money)
But I skirt it sometimes by saying
    I'm a writer or
    I'm an artist
Art they understand
There are museums—
And writing—there are books...
But poetry? Who goes?
Who buys?

It's like saying—I sit zen it's my
    job. I breathe. I emote.
Or it's being as naked
    as a mime
or a window washer on a harness
straddling a 90-foot building
during rush hour

It's a ridiculous profession
but sublime—
And to teach it?
Close to lunacy—
She's soft, touched—
But we've known this
since infancy—
She repeats words—
fashions them—
molds lines—
can't build a house
but she constructs
a lovely stanza—

The pay—hah!
Now this is lunacy absolute.
The rewards?
You—I get you—
I get 90 kids a week saying
I write, I breathe
air so fine
My heart is on fire & words &
memory
are the only balm

Susan Terence
*San Francisco*

## IN THE SCALE OF WORLDS

Sometime in the weeks after my daughter had left home,
the mother mouse found a bread basket high
in our kitchen, in the warmth, and made her home there.
She gnawed the fibers of the basket and they formed,
all around, the cloud of a white soft nest.
I had already sliced bread for lunch, and her babies
were at teat, when I pulled the top bread basket down,
puzzled by all that whiteness.

We took the basket outside and let her run
into the bergamot by the fence, all her babies attached.
Later, I remembered the chaos
of my inner life, and how paltry the weight
of it seemed, next to this. And how she and I,
most likely, would never meet up again.

Claudia Jensen Dudley
*San Francisco*

## CRUMBS

*(at the Third Grade Poetry Party)*

Alone he munches a sugar cookie.
Breaks off tiny pieces, nervously
puts them in his mouth like a wren
eating seed. *I like your poems*, I say.
Sugar spills like sand on his desk.
*You say that to everybody,*
his eyes dewed like morning petals.
I don't deny it, think of words to make
a difference, like I praise each star
and snowflake. Each bloom, all
with special glisten and heart.
I tell him how I like the mystery between
each word of his, like a quiet wind
and at the end a pop so I go *oh!*
He looks down, brushes crumbs
on the floor. No poet wants
their invention to be one
of a crowd. A *nobody* like Emily says.
I tell him I know how he feels.
That sometimes our poems seem
to run into a sea of words
so you can't tell whose is whose
as each wave is made of the same water.
*You don't know*, he says. I notice
how long his lashes are. How small he is.
I want to hug him. Instead I tell him
poems help me get through a day.
          *Like everyone's?* he asks.
          *Like yours*, I reply
as the bell rings and give him that hug, quick
and true before everyone rushes out
forever.

Perie Longo
*Santa Barbara*

# THE POSSUM

*for my daughter Talia*

> *... his round belly and his curved fingers*
> *and his black whiskers and his little dancing feet*
> —*Gerald Stern*

"It's not dead," you insisted,
rushing into the living room.
From our porch we could hear the possum
crying like a child, rasping for breath.
We saw that little body heave,
tail flipping like a whip
directly in front of our house.

Sitting upright at first, the possum
licked its injured paw.
You approached, from behind, slowly,
to encourage it out of the street.
But the possum hissed and you retreated.
Then came that icy, shattering crunch.
The second hit.

You kept crying, so I held your hand.
as watched car after car
drive over, wheel after wheel miss.
The animal hospital told us
to cover the possum with a towel,
shovel it into a box and bring it in,
careful not to get bitten because
Possums carry rabies.

We could not get near.
After you left a message
with the animal rescue mission,
I sent you to your room
and told you to forget the possum.

Later I returned to the porch
secretly hoping to find the possum
dead, so I could tell myself it was over
and go to sleep. But the possum moaned,
lifted its chest, and flipped its tail.

By morning, nothing was left
but a streak of blood.
The woman at the rescue mission
said they didn't keep track of possums,
but someone probably picked it up,
helped it or put it to sleep.

After all, it was just a possum
with pink, searchlight eyes,
a round white belly and a stick of a tail.
A hunter, curious about cities.
A quiet wanderer
we were not meant to help,
stepping into a night
you were not supposed to witness.
Belonging to no one.

Shelley Savren
*Ventura County*

## PINK ROSETTE

This child's parents
are Mexicans
who came to California
for a better life.

The fire took place
in the trailer where they lived,
in the trailer park
near the campground

that floods every winter.
The girl's hair and eyes
were saved
but her face

is just a skull
with a thin patchwork
of wrinkly grafts of skin.
The cartilage in her nose

was burned down
to the plane of her face
so that now her nostrils
are just exposed holes

into her skull.
Her mother has dressed her
in just as many lacy frills
as all the other girls

at her cousin's quinceañero,
and has clipped
a sheer pink rosette of a bow
to her black, carefully brushed hair.

**Phyllis H. Meshulam**
*Sonoma County*

# GRACE

*Portrait of Ruth Bernhard, 1935*
*Edward Weston*

sometimes a man becomes a piece of driftwood

bleached grain
sun, salt, sometimes
he strains toward sky

torsion held to

accepts
lathed angle
                accepts
a shape it is bound to

sometimes a man closes his eyes
turns away so far in the moment
he releases the shelter of being a man
dreams himself a woman
scalloped dune and shadow

becomes her
sometimes
                a landscape

holds onto itself like a root
                climbs into limb and tree
        sculpted
                muscle of wind

and skin taut with rivers

Terry Ehret
*Sonoma County*

# So Now You Know
## (Stagnation's End)

Spirit of social distortion          prison bound mainliner
Now we're even. Spread of disease. Smart went crazy
Some people will fear spirit caravan in star lite
desperation standstill stale sludge confrontations
waiting for submission's hold.      <u>all that ever mattered</u>
struggle with subterranean hysterical parasite
while out of style intoxicated jody knew the score
personal best sweet belly freak down, sweater weather
like skull kontrol      <u>deviate beyond all means</u>
ain't that america all system go   state of art.
Difficult is Easy life in a bubble look now look again.
The kitten becomes a tiger   <u>we told you not to cross us</u>.
This is medicine    hot animal     disinfect operation
came by to kill me at zero     hope     delusion.
Hell no happy go licky halo benders guinea pig
Sex mad near death experience      no more lies
notorious slaves nuzzle old time oddballs.
Flatheads rumble past     last bullet blues.
Ravishing seedy splendor still screaming
banging the drum      the pace is glacial.
Only one match left     one false move,
employ blacklist crime wave    zen guerrilla.
You and I we march hypnotic against brain death
unholy grave    payroll benefits     justice system desperation
subpoena the past revolutionaries to land somewhere
taking a chance sexadelic     means to an end.
What happens next?    Back with a vengeance:
The brave do not fear the grave.

Will Staple
*Nevada County*

## EDDIE'S FAREWELL

Eddie's ICU bed smells of exhaust fumes
from the 210, the Orange crunch, the 10
glass shards, tool box spilled, big rig gulping
Eddie, between jobs, on January rain
before imminent retirement, no one
to recognize heroes at the morgue swollen
cavity of eyes, hands on cast crusted
asleep at the wheel, escort sheep to their deaths
won't U be meek? how do I tell my house
it's orphaned? decks expand, contract with rain
God how I hate California winters
father resides in timber, hums of a
tortured architect, please doctor bring back
the carpenter that resurrected my house

Fernando D. Castro
*Los Angeles County*


## 213-310-424

Hey, I know
I'm just a number
A constantly changing number
I can't understand numbers
I can't remember numbers
So many numbers
So little time
To adjust to new numbers
A better number
I don't think so
If you care for me
You'll remember my number
I give
My number is close to up

Yvonne Mason
*Los Angeles County*

## Uses of *Vitis californica*, California Wild Grape:

In the chardonnay-warmed rays of autumn sun,
when the glassy creek reflects blood-hot leaves
from the vines' woody chains dangling
in a languorous stretch off the soft, rotting wood
of the arched footbridge, in the wine-soaked sun
reach over the bridge's rail and twist off three red leaves.
As you crush two in your hands, never mind the men climbing
the cloud-white water tower's narrow spine,
never mind the days walking past you
like leashed retrievers; today you're forgiven
lack of ambition, all the Dies you didn't Carpe;
never mind the prickly pear a fourth grader's brandished
to misspell her name in fuchsia juice
on the asphalt. Today you're forgiven her
education. If the two leaves mutate into
Was and Will Be shredded on your palm, it doesn't matter
what you do with their little pieces, having proved
the power of your hands to tear up hand-sized things.
The remaining leaf, one edge ragged from glassy-winged pests,
has the same ruby range as the other two, and invites you
to crush its blush into your memory as a dye
for anxieties, so that when you feel the press of worry,
(which is the right love, job, god), that twitch
beneath your eye, your cheeks and neck will flare in a
    way the sun
cannot resist.

Maria Melendez
*Yolo County*

# THE MORE SUBLIME NEED

Color is reflection of light not absorbed. Lime
is everything but, and tangerine's orange rind
is the disendowment of that very shade. Lately,
I wonder at the things not said. The weight we
choose to carry on, when there is no clear sign

and emotion bounces back off topic. I'm
not sure where the light goes then? In line?
In scattered fragments? Pieces of the prism beam?
Color is reflection.

If I can't adjust my angle of perception in time,
I may miss your meaning, or at least the more sublime
need you express between words. A theme
of longing for something I will never absorb seems
to be in question. How to hold and define
the pigment of love when color is reflection.

Eve West Bessier
*Yolo County*

## Rain Suite

Read together, as a trio of voices:

Voice 1 (soprano)
—*Read one time through
alone, then second time
with voice 2, then
improvise line repeats.
End after voice 3—*

Sip, Sip, Slip, lip,
sip, sip,
Sssh, shhh, shhh, wish,
this
Wish, wish, shh

(repeat)

Voice 2 (baritone)
—*After voice 1, read one
time through with voice
1, then improvise word
repeats. End after voices
1 and 3—*

blink blank, not
sock, clock, knock
not knock, not,
dark, lock, like, not
light, dot, dot,
blink, plank, not

(repeat)

90    California Poets in the Schools Statewide Anthology

Voice 3 (very clearly
articulated)
*—Begin after voices 1*
*and 2. Read forward, then*
*backward. Can repeat*
*any word or phrase—*

Hollow          sound
                              of metal
drainpipe                dripping
          water
rattling with the rain
          sound      echoing

in the light well
in the narrow
                    space
between two buildings

          this rain
in the dark
                              early morning
winter rain
before
          we open our eyes

Susan Sibbet
*San Francisco*

# SPELL

Before the alphabet was snatched up
by the mind, it belonged to the body.
Consonants huddled in the crooks
of elbow, ankle, and knee. Thriving
on gossip and potluck dinners, they built
cities with jazz clubs and intricate networks
of telephone line and highway.

But the vowels, moon-driven and drunk
on the sounds of their own voices,
lived alone, like creatures of the night,
in thatched huts and caves.

"O," thirsting most for solitude,
camped out under the belly's stars.
"I," with wingspan and vision of an eagle,
made his nest in the brows.

Like the songbird hiding its red jewel,
"U" carved out a hollow
in the isthmus of the throat. And the lioness
"E" staked claims on the mouth,
where she raised her cubs and lived
on intermittent light.

But it was "A," wild and lovely,
who holed up in the heart,
who, when each night fell, trembled in *ah*:
the *ah* of awaiting,
of Allah and amen,
the nearly inaudible *ah* of being folded up
into the arms of the lover
without a face.

Prartho Sereno
*Marin County*

## During Poetry

I sat next to Matt—though it might have been Ryan
or Thom or Jack I chose to sit by. The blue-hooded,
sweat-shirted boy who was *just Matt*.
When I asked him if he was going to write,
he sat still, his face hard, pieces of dried grass
clinging to a dirty pant leg. He began drawing dark circles
across the bottom of the lined paper in front of him.
He called it *The Nothing*, then told me
there wasn't anything inside his imagination today:
no trees, no dogs, not the storm that passed through
his backyard the night before, that tipped over
the recycling bins and trash cans his mom set out
too early in the week; the bins his dad yelled and cursed at
her for
while Matt stayed upstairs with his brother.
This morning, his mom yelled at him;
he was going to be late for school again,
and if she told him once, she told him a hundred times:
she didn't have time for this. Not today.
She didn't want to hear another word out of him.
Nothing. Got that? Absolutely nothing.
Not a single word. Just get in the car and shut the door.
Don't give me any of your lip, alright?
I don't want to write, he said again,
and filled his page with circles.

Karen Benke
*Marin County*

## Juvenile Hall

Today in Juvy
Marcel says
he's gonna sing his poem,
that two weeks ago he didn't even know what
a poem was,
that it just came out;
it just came out of him, he says
like a baby comes out of a woman,
that's what he says,
as if he knew,
he says he'd never even written a poem
before,
but this one just wants to be sung,
and he smiles crooked-like, looks
charmingly cockeyed,
places his arms on the classroom podium.
"Now, I know you're gonna want to laugh
when I sing my poem
and I'll just ask you brothers to wait,
to hold your laugh 'til I'm done,
I'm just sayin' wait."
And the big boys at the back
in their faded orange t-shirts and dark sweats,
with their shaved heads, sneers, some with
cheek scars from a quick knife, or pierced
tongues—
the boys from Richmond, from the turf and the hood,
some with biceps that seemed bolted on,
they just stared at Marcel,
watched him close his eyes like a skinny choir boy,
fill his lungs, and sing
about his girl who had the baby anyway,
and his baby girl,
how she just came out like a poem,
that sweet baby girl, how they'd made it
together then lost it;

sang until the brothers in the back wanted to sing too.
Seriously, joined in at the end.
I swear the whole class up at Juvy was stunned
when Marcel was
done with his poem—
the guards by the door, the boys at the back,
the parole officer in blue,
the nurse who dispensed small pale pills in dixie cups,
and the poetry teacher, who was all of a sudden
just one of them, one
with them, one with Marcel
and the brothers up in Juvy
because sometimes a poem
just wants to be sung.

Kathy Evans
*Marin County*


## NAPTIME IN ARCATA

Names are not important now.
Keep your eyes closed.
All these children, breathing,
and the words are going away.

Don't talk now, no questions.
Pretend you are lying by the river.
Our old hands circle their small backs,
and the words are soft piano music.

Now the hushed and darkened room
is filled with sleep.
The pet rabbit is moving among the children,
who are quiet now, and the words are gone.

Daniel Zev Levinson
*Humboldt County*

# LESSON PLANS & ESSAY

# Talking to the Ancestors

A sense of the past and of place form the dual nodes of inspiration I want to invoke in this lesson that I've taught to fourth and fifth graders. I use my own poem, "Patterns of the Past," to illustrate the images that may arise from considering not only the personality traits, work and community (stable or changing) of one's forebears, but also the geography and climate — those highly tangible elements of life — that mold a person in sensate ways.

## Patterns of the Past
### (for Finland)

Bread
and the small white fish of the lake.

Do you go with me
to the red pine-wood church?
Thin white wafers
at the altar,
dark drink to cleanse the soul.

Wind in the white nights
unnerves the silent glow.
Warm the bones
white under the flesh,
at sauna‚Äôs hot stones,
at the kitchen‚Äôs heated stove.

The family gathers in the large room.
Silence shows respect.
Stories and singing lighten the time.
Berry bread, nut bread,
sugar in the coffee,
cheese baked black on the oven‚Äôs
lowest shelf.

Learn to be
quiet as a winter mouse,
learn to fly
outdoors in the long summer sun.

Store green under your skin,
weave fire into the rug.
Red cushions in white snow,
bells under black branches.

**Grace Grafton**

A week before the lesson, I ask classroom teachers to send home a hand-out that helps students interview their grandparents (preferably) or their parents about where they grew up — specifically about landscape, weather patterns, what kinds of foods they typically ate, family traditions, what they did for fun and work as children and adults. When we write the poems, students may refer to the answers for the details of their poem.

Beginning the lesson, I ask students to imagine living two hundred years ago. What do we have now that folks didn't have then? How did people spend their evenings (entertain themselves)? How did people get food, cook, clean? How was the clothing different, especially in countries other than the United States, where some of their ancestors might have lived? We might write an example group poem about the group ancestor from two hundred years ago.

To write their individual poems, I suggest that students think first about the place, the weather, the foods their interviewee told them about, so we can get a sense, from their poem, about their ancestor's sensate, everyday life. I suggest, for the second part, that they might speak to their ancestor (I make clear that an ancestor is any family member who has lived before them, so a parent qualifies), either telling the person conversationally what their life was like, "You wore knee-socks and a wool cap for the snowy weather," or ask them questions. The question method allows students to expand the poem beyond the information they received from the interview. "Did you like to read, the way I do?"

"The way I do" provides a third aspect to the poem. I suggest they compare their own life to the life of their ancestor. Some ways the same, some different. "Did I get my hazel eyes and love of skating from you, or did you have to work so hard you never got to skate?"

## THE PAST

Rice.
and the sound of tea simmering for
breakfast.
Bikes speeding past the small
window
small lights to light the small
kitchen where his mom gives him rice.
Grandma pours him boiling tea as
he stares at the many hills in
Hong Kong. The Big City surrounds
him as he leaves to go to
school.
Dad did you play an instrument?
did you also wish to fly?

**Melissa Lee**
*Lakeshore School*

*— Grace Grafton, San Francisco*

## ALLEGORY RUBS THE SLEEP FROM HER EYES

Last year in my CPITS workshops, I tried to revive allegory, a technique I had been discouraged from using when I was in college. "It's like reading Spenser or Bunyan," one of my college classmates had said with a grimace. For a while after that, I believed allegory was not cool.

But to say that allegory had died would be to go too far.

Even in Billy Collins' poem "The Death of Allegory," the "tall abstractions" don't die; they merely retire to sleep just over the hill often seen on the last page of storybooks. Collins does in fact awaken History in the poem "The Lesson." History is an old man who snores. Without asking, the narrator borrows History's coat to go to the store and when he returns with milk, History angrily takes his coat back and checks the pocket for a missing queen or battle. The abstraction's petulant mood is downright human.

The mistake in my college allegory was trying to make a human stand for a concept rather than letting the concept stand for the human. The distinction might seem slight, but while bringing abstractions to humans feels arbitrary, bringing the human back to the abstraction feels honest. Characters as concepts tend to flatten in an inhuman way; concepts as flawed characters take on a human dimension and are funny.

A recurring challenge for student-poets is balancing the degree of abstract and concrete in a poem. Because the allegory renders the abstract as a character, it sets up a basic writing challenge to get the human into the poem. For my workshop on allegory, I remind the class about how we need to use people and things to discover and show feeling. Then I read "The Lesson." We brainstorm a bunch of abstractions on the board. I tell them to pick one that reminds them of themselves and then draft poems in which the abstraction becomes a person who interacts with things in a specific place in the world: who says and does things.

Many students discovered that it was good to have the narrator interact with the abstraction, as in Peter-Jon Mueller's poem below.

## Forgetful On the Couch

One afternoon, I found Forgetfulness watching TV.
He was eating pizza without a plate on the new carpet.
There were muddy footprints in the hall and
my mom's wedding glass shattered on the floor.
When I saw this mess I said, "Forgetfulness,
look, you're supposed to do your report tomorrow."
"I forget," he said.
"You're grounded, you're watching TV, and
you know you're not supposed to eat in this room without
        a plate."
He said, "I'm sorry with my whole heart."
Next thing I know he's making muddy footprints down the hall
To the freezer for ice cream to spoil his appetite.

**Peter-Jon Mueller**
*Grade 5, San Pasqual Union, Escondido*
*Teacher: Wendy Snapp*

Randy Hanson's variation on "The Lesson" finds history much more animated and the dénouement is surreal and totally cool.

## Jumping History

History jumps on a trampoline,
doing summersaults and front flips.
He jumps into space like an astronaut going to Jupiter.
When he came back down,
a blustering cat was jumping, hissing and meowing.
It swallowed History and went on,
its tail waving back and forth
like a pen writing fast.

**Randy Hanson**
*Grade 5, San Pasqual Union*
*Teacher: Patricia Matson*

Several of the students decided not to make the abstraction a character but a tangible thing, a feeling you could touch.

## PASSING SADNESS

One day I was feeling sad,
so I took the sadness out and
threw it down the hill really hard.
But there were people having a party.
The sadness hit someone who went inside.
She started crying. I knocked on her door
and said I was sorry.
All she said was, "Don't do it again."
She gave me back the sadness,
so I ran home crying just like that other girl.

McKenna Plant
Grade 2, San Pasqual Union
Teacher: Teri MacDonald

— *Brandon Cesmat, San Diego*

Works Cited: Collins, Billy. *The Apple That Astonished Paris.*
Pittsburgh: U of Pittsburgh Press, 1988 and *Questions About Angels.* Pittsburgh: U of Pittsburgh Press, 1991.

## A BANQUET OF WORDS

I start this lesson by talking about eating many different kinds of food. I have them imagine they are at the beach in a bathing suit and can get as messy as they like because they can go swimming when they get dirty. Some of the things we talk about are pizza: how the cheese stretches out, watermelon with the juice dripping down your chin, sucking up long strands of spaghetti, licking a dripping ice cream cone, or eating barbecued ribs, or rolled tacos.

As they are talking I put some of the verbs like dripping, stretching, spitting, on the board. We also talk about emotions: happiness, loneliness, pain, and put those words on the board also. Then we discuss some of the things that poets write about such as the moon, sea, mountains, snowflakes, and also the etiquette of eating with forks and knives, napkins, plates, and put them up on the board too so that they have a great banquet of words to choose from.

Then I have the students read aloud "Eating Poetry" by Mark Strand, "How to Eat a Poem" by Eve Merriam, and Victor Valle's "Comida" so they can hear how other poets write about the same subject. I emphasize the fact that they should have a lot of fun with it. The poems by the younger grades seem fresher and yet the poem by Carlos was written just before lunch and I think that motivated his very sensuous poem, while Shawn's takes on the aspect of a recipe.

### IF I EAT A POEM

If I eat a poem
It will taste nasty, sometimes
And good at others
I will spit out words from my mouth
Like watermelon seeds
The poem will taste like
Birds, stars, hair and wood
Wood is hard to bite

It will leave splinters in my mouth
Splinters will hurt
Then I will eat a star
Because I don't know
How stars taste.

Kenny Martinez
Grade 3, Palmer Way Elementary
Classroom teacher: Melissa Harley

## How to Eat a Poem

If I ate a poem
I'd taste tender chicken
With big flakes of cheese
And toppings of chocolate and tomato sauce
And noodles sprinkled with catsup
Mustard, barbecue sauce and lots of Chile
It would swirl in my mouth
With a shout of about everything
I'd eat a poem til I got full
I'd eat with my hands
Or even better, mix everything in a giant bowl
And then jump into the pool of poems
I'd slurp and gobble everything down
As if I was a vulture and could eat a lot
I'd play in the spices
And swim through the sauces
While I slurp
That's how I'd eat a poem!

Carlos Navarro
*Grade 6, Valle Lindo Elementary*
*Classroom teacher: Frank Luzzaro*

## A LITTLE EXTRA SPICE

Smash the poem together
sprinkle morsels of salt on it
to make it more
inviting
Skim the poem
with a delicate feather
to soften it up so it doesn't
pierce or confuse my brain
Add sweet fragrances of violets
to its bland surface
to make it more presentable
to the nose
Slit the edges to fix its flaws
so it's superlative
to the naked eye
Add some laughter, yelling, crying
to connect all of its
luscious flavors
Bake it all in the oven
of imagination.

Shawn Wilcox
Grade 7, Mesa Verde Middle
Classroom teacher: Daniel Fleming

This lesson plan is also a time to explore cultural diversity
which is so evident in the foods we eat. Oftentimes students
think spaghetti, pizza, tacos, and burritos are American foods.
Then I ask them where gumbo, fortune cookies, or tabouli come
from so they can see how diverse our culture really is.

—*Glory Foster, San Diego*

# Wishing You A Propitious 4699 Year

According to my mother, one of my earliest sentences was "I can't wait till I'm 35." While my friends wanted Barbies and plastic horses, I longed for experience, awareness, wisdom — the kind of self-possession that only comes through time. Good or bad, this expectant mantra has dogged me through my life, but I didn't take it seriously till my thirtieth birthday when a voice came into my head while I was meditating and whispered "five more years."

Well, those five more years culminated this year. I was contemplating this anticlimactic detail when I contacted the English teacher at Pacific Charter School to set up my poetry visit. When we looked at the calendar for available dates, I noticed the Chinese New Year fell during the week we both had open. Gong Hay Fat Choy. Chinese Lunar New Year #4699. It was perfect: a great way for a 35-year-old snake to usher in the Year of the Snake. I decided to create a special three days of poetry centered around the customs and traditions of the Chinese New Year.

About two weeks before my classes were to start, I hit the Internet. Nearly seventy pages of text and twenty classic Chinese poems later, I made myself stop; it would take at least 15 lessons for me to share all the fun stuff I'd gathered. It took some doing, but eventually I organized the material into three lessons: Chinese Red Couplets; Origin Stories; and Recipes For A Snake Year Celebration. For atmosphere and effect, I put together three Chinese-flavored outfits — all in New Year's red of course.

### Chinese Red Couplets
"May you have a mouth as sharp as a dagger but a heart as soft as tofu."

I began this lesson with an introduction into the Chinese New Year — what it is, when it occurs, who celebrates it, why — and after explaining that New Years is the biggest holiday of the year in China, I asked the students what the biggest holiday in America is (all said Christmas or Chanukah). I then had them give me examples of things their families traditionally do to prepare for the holidays. We compared this list to the new years preparations in china (shopping, paying off debt, traveling to visit relatives, cleaning, and decorating their houses for the coming celebration.)

I explained that, according to Chinese tradition, everything associated with the New Year should represent good fortune, and decorations are an important part of this tradition, especially a type of hanging scrolls called Red Couplets. Revealing a Red Couplet hanging scroll I made especially for the lesson, I asked the students if they knew what a couplet was (at least one student in every class, even in the younger grades, knew the answer — hurray!). I added that Red Couplets are special Chinese good luck sayings written in gold on red paper and hung on doors for good luck. We made an inventory of typical good luck themes, such as praise of nature, longevity, wealth, happiness, good marriages, lots of children, etc. Next, we made a shopping list for images related to each of these themes. Finally, it was time for students to write their own red couplets (which, of course, ended up much longer than two lines):

## WELCOME SNAKE

May this year bring you
The easy peace
Of a ridge stream
Bubbling and twisting
Through ferns
Rocks formed so long ago

May you always notice
Tiny mushroom polka dots
Brown and spindly
Caps reaching for sky
Like baby fireworks
Bursting from deep
Beneath the earth

When they were done, students turned their poems into hanging scrolls and by the end of the day, the doors and windows were decorated for the celebration to come.

### Origin Poems

On the second day of class, New Year's Eve, I began by asking students why the Chinese chose the color red for their hanging scroll decorations (students said Happiness, Good Luck, Good Fortune). After I commended them on their memory, I then went on to explain that red also frightens off the ancient monster "Nian." I asked if they wanted to know more about "Nian" and, as expected, I got a collective "YES!" So I told them the legend of Nian, the tale of a monster who tormented people around New Year's, destroying crops and homes until an old man came and saved the day by tricking Nian into leaving the villagers alone.

I wrapped up the Nian myth by explaining that the Chinese phrase "Guo Nian", which used to mean "Survive the Nian" has now become "Celebrate the (New) Year," since the word "guo" in Chinese is has two meanings — to "pass-over" and "observe" — and Nian is simply the word for "year." The custom of putting up red paper and firing fire-crackers in celebration originally came from the need to scare away Nian.

I next asked students if they knew any origin stories associated with American holidays, and they mentioned Arctic shamans, spring fertility rites, pagan new years, generous indigenous peoples, and the Star Spangled Banner. I passed out several "origin poem" examples and after we read and discussed them, I invited students to come up with poems reflecting their personal creation stories — the earliest stories they remember hearing about themselves — even if they don't remember these events personally.

### BUDDHA BABY

when I was born
Mama says I had three chins
a Buddha belly
cheeks red as zinfandel
first and only
she says I slipped through her
like an acrobat on a slide
my cry eager, raucous

baby toes tumbling their soft round rocks
into the next river
all of me wiggling from doctor hands to hers
proud smile entering my gaze
in the one motionless moment
it took for my elbow to leap and dive
into her eye

this is why my newborn albums
are filled with shots of me without her
me sleeping in a basket of willowy arms
me laughing on the knee of homemade Capris
me, already a circus clown
with an anonymous mother
a three ringed love framed
by the delicate edges of southern vanity

### Recipes For A Snake Year Celebration

Finally, New Year's Day had arrived, and looking around the room, I saw a sea of red sweatshirts and sweaters: to my delight, many of the kids remembered me saying that Chinese children dress entirely in red on New Years Day. I passed out peanuts (in their shells) and had students guess what they symbolized (long life), then told them about some of the traditional New Year's foods and how they are all associated with a symbol or desire for good luck (for instance, Black moss seaweed is a homonym for exceeding in wealth).

I gave them a brief explanation on the lunar calendar and the Chinese zodiac, including the reasons 2001 was the year of the metal snake. I then shared the legend of the zodiac (another origin story, I reminded them) and, bringing back the food analogy, brought up Chinese New Year's foods and how these special dishes made me wonder what kind of ingredients went into baking up a good New Year. Again, I had students make a shopping list of words used to direct cooks (add, mix, stir), measurements (tbsp, tsp, pinch), cooking utensils (pots, baking dish, spoon), and results/surprises (delicious, burned, golden brown, al dente). When this was finished I assigned a "Recipe For the

Snake Year" and had the students draw a spiral/snake on a paper plate (head in the middle) and write the poem along the spiral (beginning at the snake's head), decorate and cut out their snakes, and hang them up in the classroom.

## RECIPE FOR A GOOD METAL SNAKE YEAR

Take a cup of books
Fold in a good teacher
Stir really well
Let sit till recess

Then add a tsp. of sugar venom
A month of rain
Soak into a lucky smelling perfume

When ready, bring mixture to a boil
throw in a metal rose
Stir with lots of breath
(it will become thick and dreamy)
Pour all ingredients into a waffle iron until scaly

Sprinkle on a year of happiness and money
Top with firecrackers and balloons
Eat every day or when hungry

(especially until the full moon)

The monkeys, roosters, dogs & rats
Pacific Charter School, 1-3 grade class


I still don,t know if this year is going to bring me any extraordinary fireworks or not. But it doesn't really matter. Not only did I get through my early thirties without aging worries, but all of us at the Pacific Charter School certainly got a great New Year's celebration — and some fabulous poems — out of the deal.

*— Blake More, Mendocino*

# BIBLIOGRAPHY

## WEB SITES

**Where you can find information:**

inkspot.com
For Young Writers: Market Info
www.inkspot.com/young/market/

**Where you can publish students' work:**

Chapbooks for Learning
www.chapbooks.com
Note: This is not an e-zine, but an on-line company that uses the technology to publish old-fashioned books.

Cyberkids
ages 7-12
www.cyberkids.com/we/html/kids.html

Cyberteens
ages 13-19
www.cyberteens.com

Human Beams-Young Minds
ages 10-18
www.humanbeams.com/young/index.html

KidNews
all ages, but mainly elementary grades
www.kidnews.com/

KidPub
no ages specified
www.Kidpub.org/kidpub

Kids' Space
younger children
www.kids-space.org/index.html

Kidstory
all ages, not very good prose but better poetry
www.kidstory.com

MidLink Magazine
middle school and some high school
www.cs.ucf.edu/~MidLink/

The Sidewalk's End
no ages specified
www3.cybercities.com/s/sidewalk/ezine.html

Writes of Passage
12-19
www.writes.org/index.html

(Thanks to Susanna Lang for this list.)

## POETRY BIBLIOGRAPHY FOR YOUNG ADULTS

Adoff, Arnold, ed. *I Am the Darker Brother: An Anthology of Modern Poems by African Americans.*

Berry, James. *When I Dance: Poems by James Berry.*

Blum, Joshua, ed. *United States of Poetry.*

Brown, Kurt, ed. *Drive, They Said: Poems about Americans and Cars.*

Carlson, Lori, ed. *Cool Salsa: Bilingual Poems.*

Carroll, Joyce and Edward Wilson, ed. *Poetry After Lunch: Poems to Read Aloud.*

Dahl, Roald. *Fractured Fairy Tales.*

Duffy, Carol Ann, ed. *I Wouldn't Thank You for a Valentine: Poems for Young Feminists.*

Dunning, Stephen, Edward Leuders, and Hugh Smith, eds. *Reflections on a Gift of Watermelon Pickle...And Other Modern Verse* and *Some Haystacks Don't Even Have Any Needle...And Other Complete Modern Poems.*

Fleishman, Paul. *I Am Phoenix: Poems for Two Voices.*

Fletcher, Ralph. *Room Enough for Love.*

Frost, Robert, and Peter Koeppen, illus. *A Swinger of Birches: Poems of Robert Frost for Young People.*

Giovanni, Nikki, ed. *Shimmy Shimmy Shimmy Like My Sister Kate: Looking at the Harlem Renaissance through Poems.*

Glenn, Mel, *Class Dismissed! High School Poems, Class Dismissed II, The Taking of Room 114, Jump Ball: Basketball Season,* and *Who Killed Mr. Chippendale?*

Gordon, Ruth, ed. *Pierced by a Ray of Sun: Poems about the Times We Feel Alone,* and *Under All Silences: Shades of Love.*

Greenfield, Eloise. *Honey, I Love, and Other Love Poems.*

Hempel, Amy and Jim Shepard ed. *Unleashed: Poems by Writers' Dogs.*

Hesse, Karen. *Out of the Dust.*

Hirschfelder, Arlene B., and Beverly R. Singer, eds. *Rising Voices: Writings of Young Native Americans.*

Hull, Robert, ed. *Breaking Free: An Anthology of Human Rights Poetry.*

Johnson, James Weldon, *The Creation.*

Kerdian, David, ed. *Beat Voices: An anthology of Beat Poetry.*

Koch, Kenneth, and Kate Farrell, eds. *Talking to the Sun: An Illustrated Anthology of Poems for Young People.*

Larrick, Nancy, ed. *Bring Me All of Your Dreams.*

Livingston, Myra Cohn, ed. *A Time to Talk: Poems of Friendship*, and *Call Down the Moon: Poems of Music.*

Lyne, Sandford, ed. *Ten-Second Rainshowers: Poems by Young People.*

Marcus, Leonard S., ed. *Lifelines: A Poetry Anthology Patterned on the Stages of Life.*

Medearis, Angela Shelf. *Skin Deep, and Other Teenage Reflections.*

Merriam, Eve. *Inner City Mother Goose.*

Miller, E. Ethelbert, ed. *In Search of Color Everywhere.*

Morrison, Lillian, ed. *Rhythm Road: Poems to Move to.*

Nye, Naomi Shihab and Paul B. Janeczko, ed. *I Feel a Little Jumpy Around You.*

Nye, Naomi Shihab, ed. *This Same Sky: A Collection of Poems from Around the World.*

Peacock, Molly, Elise Paschen, Neil Neches ed. *Poetry in Motion : 100 Poems from the Subways and Buses.*

Rosenberg, Liz, ed. *The Invisible Ladder: An Anthology of Contemporary American Poems for Young Readers.*

Try these websites for other poetry bibliographies:

www.clpgh.org/ein/ya/yapoetry.html
www.nypl.org/branch/teen/earth.html

## Periodicals for Students

(Compiled by Maureen Kerl DiSavino)

Dear Students-Poets,

Here are some magazines that accept children's finished poems—poems that you have rewritten, typed out, and properly spelled and checked over. Send your best work. When you send your poems to a magazine, remember:

1. Include a cover sheet with your name and home address and phone number; your grade, school, school address, and phone number; and teacher's name if appropriate;

2. Send a self-addressed, stamped envelope (SASE) that's big enough and has enough postage, so that the editors can return your work if they don't choose to use it. Don't be discouraged! Many writers get rejection slips, even your own poet-teachers;

3. Type your full name, address, school, and age on each poem. If your poem is more than one page, put this information on each page;

4. Be patient. Good luck! Keep trying! Keep writing!

*Children's Digest*, Box 567 Indianapolis, IN 46206. Publishes eight times a year. Requires a letter from your parent or teacher stating that the work is originial. Payment in copies and special subscription rate. Prints about 30 poems per year. Send SASE. Responds in eight to ten weeks. Editor's advice: Keep trying!

*Creative Kids*, Box 6448 Mobile, AL 36660. Publishes eight times a year, ages 5-18. Each piece must be labeled with the student's name, birth date, address, and school address. Responds in four weeks, pays in free magazine. A recent school picture is a good idea. Sometimes an accepted work will take a long time to get into print, depending on the theme of your poem. Editor's advice: Keep trying!

*Highlights for Children*, 803 Church St. Honesdale, PA 18431. Publishes 11 times a year, prints 10 to 15 poems per issue. Also publishes adult articles. Tries to respond in four weeks. Grades K-12. Put your age on the poems along with your name and address.

*Merlyn's Pen*, PO Box 1058, East Greenwich, CT 02818. Publishes four times a year. Accepts all forms of writing and artwork from students in grades 7-12. Cover sheet and SASE required. Responds to all submissions, usually within ten weeks. Payment: three copies of the magazine.

*Stone Soup, The Magazine for Children*, Children's Art Foundation, Box 83, Santa Cruz, CA 95063. Publishes five times a year. Accepts poems, stories, artwork, and book reviews by children. Age limit: 13. Responding time: four weeks. payment in copies and cash. Editor's advice: read a few issues to find out if your work is suitable for the magazine. Send a SASE.

## Classic Texts About Teaching Poetry and Poetry-Writing to Children

*Children Write Poetry: A Creative Approach*, 1951, 1967, Flora J. Arnstein, Dover Books

*Creative Power*, Hughes Mearnes, 1929, Dover Books

*Getting From Here to There: Writing and Reading Poetry*, Florence Grossman, Boynton/Cook Publishers

*Sound and Sense:An Introduction to Poetry*, 1956, Laurence Peffine, Harcourt Brace Jovanovich

*Wishes, Lies, and Dreams*, 1970, and Rose, Where Did You Get That Red?, 1973, Kenneth Koch, Vintage Books, Random House

## RECOMMENDED TEXTS

*The Art of Writing:A Guide for Poets, Students, and Readers*, by William Packard, St. Martin's Press, NY © 1992. Karl Shapiro writes that this is a classic among poetry writing how-to books. It includes not only the history of poetry and poetic devices, but writing challenges to develop form and style, and remarks by dozens of poets.

*The Discovery of Poetry*, Frances Mayes, © 1987, Harcourt Brace Jovanovich. A comprehensive and thorough text on the reading and writing of poetry, with a clear introduction to poetry's art and craft.

*For the Good of the Earth and Sun*, Georgia Heard, © 1989, Heinemann. A very good text for teaching poetry to grades K-12. Many exercises and process notes. Offers a method for teaching poetry that respects the intelligence and originality of both teacher and student.

*In the Palm of Your Hand*, The Poet's Portable Workshop, Steve Kowit, © 1995, Tilbury House, Publishers. "A lively and illuminating guide for the practicing poet," as the cover states, with many lessons that can be easily adapted to teaching young poets.

*poemcrazy: freeing your life with words*, Susan Wooldridge, © 1996, Clarkson Potter. Excellent book by long-time CPITS poet-teacher, filled with many practice lessons, as well as observations on how poetry is found, and how it fits into everyday life. Important for its attitude as well as its content.

*The Poet's Companion*, Kim Addonizio and Dorianne Laux, © 1997, WW Norton & Co. A compendium of poetry lessons on craft and subjects (Sex, Death, Love, the Family, etc.) drawn from the authors' teaching experience. Includes interviews with contemporary poets, and model poems.

*The Poetry Connection:An Anthology of Contemporary Poems with Ideas to Stimulate Children's Writing*, Kinereth Gensler and Nina Nyhart, © 1978. An excellent double anthology of adult and children's poetry, cross-indexed with lessons and teaching approaches.

*A Poetry Handbook*, Mary Oliver, © 1994, Harcourt Brace & Co. A simple and exquisite explanation of craft by a foremost American poet.

*Rising Voices, A Guide to Young Writers' Resources*, Second Edition, Poets & Writers, Inc., New York. Up-to-date information about the best opportunities (including summer camps) for poets, fiction writers, and playwrights, K-12. A new section lists web sites and other on-line areas for young writers.

*Starting with Little Things, A Guide to Writing Poetry in the Classroom*, Ingrid Wendt. Oregon Arts Foundation, 2111 Front St., NE, Ste. 210, Salem, OR 97303. A well-organized and practical handbook with 15 lessons, commentary, and poems by Oregon writers.

*Writing Poetry*, Barbara Drake, © 1983, Harcourt Brace Jovanovich. A solid handbook with 12 chapters full of teaching ideas, suggestions for writing, sample poems, a section on publishing, and a short bibliography.

## BOOK SOURCES

California Poets in the Schools
870 Market St., Ste. 1148
San Francisco, CA 94102
(415) 399-1565

California Poets in the Schools features yearly anthologies of student and poet-teacher poetry from 1981 to the present. The last five publications are *Listen to the Wild*, © 1996, *Belonging to California*, © 1997, *Wilderness of Dreams*, © 1998, *A Flame of Words*, © 1999, and *100 Parades*, © 2000. Each of these anthologies also contains lessons and essays on the art of teaching poetry writing. (Availability of some anthologies may be limited.)

OYATE
2702 Matthews St.
Berkeley, CA 94702
(510) 848-6700

An organization of elders, artists, activists, educators, and writers who have come together to bring the real histories of the indigenous peoples of this continent to the attention of all Americans. Texts, resources, books, fiction, poetry, children's books and materials written and illustrated by Native people. Write for a catalogue, which includes storytelling work by Joseph Bruchac and poetry by Mary Tallmountain. There's also a book called Basic Skills Caucasian Americans Workbook.

Small Press Traffic
766 Valencia Street
San Francisco, CA 94110

Small Press Traffic is an excellent source of literary magazines and small press publications of poetry, most of which you can't find in larger bookstores.

*Teaching Tolerance*
Southern Poverty Law Center
400 Washington St.
Montgomery, AL 36104

A quarterly magazine distributed free to all teachers (just write for it on letterhead) from the organization which has filed successful lawsuits against the KKK and Aryan Nation. This is full of valuable lesson ideas from other teachers; kids art and writing; and also a growing array of teaching tools (videos, posters, book lists) all on the subject of human tolerance. Inspired and inspiring.

Teachers and Writers Collaborative
5 Union Square West
New York, NY 10003-3306

Teachers and Writers has an excellent catalogue of books about teaching writing, and publishes many of them. They also put out a magazine with articles, lessons, and essays about teaching writing. Highly recommended as a resource.

VIDEO SOURCE

The American Poetry Archives
The Poetry Center
San Francisco State University
1600 Holloway Ave.
San Francisco, CA 94132
(415) 338-1056

The American Poetry Archives rents and sells videotapes of all the poetry readings made by the Poetry Center since 1973, as well as of readings and interviews from the Lannan Literary Series, and of the outtakes of the 1960's NET series USA: Poetry. These consist of extensive interviews with major poets of that time, such as Charles Olson and Anne Sexton. An excellent way for students to see a wide range of varying backgrounds, styles, and voices. Catalogue available.

# CPITS Board of Directors

CALIFORNIA
POETS IN THE
SCHOOLS

# THERE'S NO BETTER INVESTMENT

**CALIFORNIA POETS IN THE SCHOOLS**

CPITS needs your support. There are many ways you can help.

- Support your local poets!
- Encourage the creative writing, critical thinking, and self esteem of our children.
- Take time for your own poetry.
- Share and affirm the diversity of California by insuring that our schools bring culturally competent poets and multicultural materials into the classroom.
- Build partnerships between schools, the community, and poets and artists.

...*And of course*, become a *Friend of CPITS*. Please join at whatever level you can afford.

- ☐ $10,000  Angel
- ☐ $5,000  Laureate
- ☐ $1,000  Benefactor
- ☐ $500  Patron
- ☐ $350  Leader
- ☐ $100  Sponsor
- ☐ $50  Associate/Organization
- ☐ $35  Contributor

Name _____

Address _____

City/State/Zip _____

Phone (day) _____ - _____ (eve) _____ - _____

Signature _____ Date _____

VISA/MC # ☐☐☐☐ ☐☐☐☐ ☐☐☐☐ ☐☐☐☐  Expires on _____

Contributions of $35 or more will receive the current edition of CPITS' Statewide Anthology — the best of the amazing poetry children produce in CPITS' workshops annually across the state. PLEASE MAKE CHECKS PAYABLE TO:

**CPITS, 870 Market Street, Suite 1148, San Francisco, CA 94102.**
*Your contribution to CPITS is tax-deductible.*

- ☐ Please send me more information on CPITS.
- ☐ I am a teacher. I teach at _____

  in the county of _____

  school address _____

  phone _____ - _____

- ☐ I'd like to sponsor a poet residency for our school.
- ☐ I'd like to volunteer. Please contact me.
- ☐ My employer (or spouse's employer) will match my contribution to California Poets in the Schools.
- ☐ Enclosed is my signed matching gift form.

For more information, please call us at 415.399.1565 or toll free at 877-CPITS64 or e-mail: info@cpits.org

**THANK YOU!**